A PRACTICAL GUIDE FOR CRISIS RESPONSE IN OUR SCHOOLS

Fifth Edition

a publication of

The American Academy of Experts in Traumatic Stress®

New York

Published by

The American Academy of Experts in Traumatic Stress®

Administrative Offices, 368 Veterans Memorial Highway, Commack, New York 11725
Tel. (631) 543-2217 • (631) 543-6977 • Automated Fax Back System (516) 771-8103
www.schoolcrisisresponse.com • www.atsm.org
www.traumatic-stress.org • www.aaets.org

ISBN: 0-9674762-3-2

A PRACTICAL GUIDE FOR CRISIS RESPONSE IN OUR SCHOOLS

Fifth Edition

a publication of

The American Academy of Experts in Traumatic Stress®

The American Academy of Experts in Traumatic Stress is a multidisciplinary network of professionals committed to the advancement of intervention for survivors of trauma. The Academy's international membership includes individuals from over 200 professions in the health-related fields, emergency services, criminal justice, forensics, law, business and education. With members in every state of the United States and over 45 foreign countries, the Academy is now the largest organization of its kind in the world. For information about Membership, the *International Registry*, the Academy's Board Certification Programs in Traumatic Stress Specialties, Certification in Acute Traumatic Stress Management (ATSM), the Diplomate Credential, Fellowship and other benefits of Membership with the Academy, please contact:

The American Academy of Experts in Traumatic Stress®

Administrative Offices, 368 Veterans Memorial Highway, Commack, New York 11725
Tel. (631) 543-2217 • Fax (631) 543-6977 • Automated Fax Back System (516) 771-8103
www.schoolcrisisresponse.com
www.traumatic-stress.org
www.atsm.org
www.aaets.org

A Practical Guide for Crisis Response in Our Schools is published by The American Academy of Experts in Traumatic Stress. It is offered with the understanding that the Academy does not practice medicine or psychology, or provide direct or indirect patient/client care. This guide should not take the place of competent professional services. Additional copies may be obtained by utilizing the order form provided in the back of this publication.

ADMINISTRATION AND MEMBERS OF THE BOARD OF SCIENTIFIC & PROFESSIONAL ADVISORS

For the children and their families...

The American Academy of Experts in Traumatic Stress®

Administrative Offices, 368 Veterans Memorial Highway, Commack, New York 11725
Tel. (631) 543-2217 • Fax (631) 543-6977 • Automated Fax Back System (516) 771-8103
www.aaets.org • www.traumatic-stress.org • www.traumaticstressresources.org
www.atsm.org • www.survivors-thrivers.org • www.schoolcrisisresponse.com
FEDERAL IDENTIFICATION NO. 11-3285203

Dear Fellow Educator,

With the changing spirit of our times, school districts across our nation have been charged with the responsibility of developing comprehensive school crisis response plans. These plans typically focus on the *structure* of crisis response—in the aftermath of a tragedy. For example, they address such issues as who will serve as members of a school crisis response team? What are the specific roles of team members? And, how will information be shared with the school family?

Although these structured plans have been developed and implemented by our school districts, little attention has been given to the *process* of school crisis response. For example, once students have been assembled in a lounge, library or other counseling venue, what is done to help them? What is the goal of early intervention? Who is truly prepared to address emergent psychological needs?

This new edition of *A Practical Guide for Crisis Response in Our Schools* is a dramatically expanded publication that provides a structure and process for effectively managing the wide spectrum of school-based crises—from the seemingly mundane to the most severe. **School crisis response is no longer delegated to school administrators and members of a school crisis response team. Effective crisis management is the responsibility of *all* educators.**

This publication introduces and incorporates a practical and effective strategy for addressing the emotional needs of people *during* traumatic events, **Acute Traumatic Stress Management** (ATSM). ATSM does not require caregivers to be mental health practitioners. Rather, ATSM can empower all educators by providing a "road map" to keep people functioning and mitigate long-term emotional suffering.

A Practical Guide for Crisis Response in Our Schools is an invaluable resource *in preparation for*, and *during*, actual crisis situations. It has established a meaningful standard for our nation's schools. This publication additionally aims to prepare professionals who seek to achieve **Board Certification in School Crisis Response**™. An application and examination may be found in the back of this guide.

By reaching our school families early, during times of crisis, we can reestablish a productive educational process and prevent the acute stress reactions of today from becoming the chronic stress disorders of tomorrow.

Sincerely,

Mark D. Lerner, Ph.D.
President

Table of Contents

CHAPTER ONE

Introduction

What is a crisis?

A crisis is a traumatic event that seriously disrupts our coping and problem-solving abilities. It is typically unpredicted, volatile in nature and may even threaten our survival. A crisis can present a drastic and tragic change in our environment. This change is generally unwanted and frightening, and may leave us with a sense of vulnerability and helplessness. **Although crises may initially have a negative impact on people, it is important to recognize that crises present opportunities. They are decisive, crucial experiences that can ultimately lead to growth.**

What kinds of crises are impacting our schools?

The school setting is not immune to crisis situations. Although some recent trends regarding violence, substance abuse and teen pregnancy are promising, negative events continue to impact the school environment. Consider the following:

- In a 2001 study of high school students, 17.4 % responded that they carried a weapon to school during the 30 days preceding the survey (MMWR, 2002).

- In 1999, one in six teachers reported being the victim of violence in or near their school, whereas one in nine teachers reported such an experience in 1994. In 1999, students ages 12 through 18 were the victims of approximately 2.5 million crimes at school (U.S. Department of Justice, 2001).

- Suicide is the third leading cause of death among people 15 to 24 years of age, following accidents and homicide (National Center for Health Statistics, 2000). The suicide rate among 15 to 19 year old adolescents has increased by as much as 300% between 1950 and 1990 (American Academy of Pediatrics, 2000).

- Motor vehicle accidents are the leading cause of death for 15 to 20 year old individuals. In 2000, 3,594 drivers 15 to 20 years old were killed with an additional 348,000 injured in such crashes (NHTSA, 2000).

> • The number of cases of Acquired Immune Deficiency Syndrome (AIDS) and Human Immunodeficiency Virus (HIV) reported each year for individuals between the ages of 13 and 19 continues to increase significantly. Through 2001, the U.S. Centers for Disease Control and Prevention (CDC) reports 4,219 cumulative cases of AIDS among children ages 13 through 19 with the number of teens living with HIV estimated to be considerably higher (NIH, 2002).

Today's school districts must contend with reactions to new types of trauma. For example, hostage-taking, sniper attacks, murders, terrorist activities and bombings were almost nonexistent in the schools thirty years ago. Noteworthy is that there is a strong indication in the literature that the effects of these deliberately-caused disasters, of "intentional human design" (IHD), and resultant victimization are worse than naturally-caused disasters (Baum et al., 1983; Ursano et al., 1994). **Despite considerable social, familial and educational changes, most educators do not receive specific training in responding to the diversity of crisis situations.**

Specific events include, but are certainly not limited to:

- an accident involving a student or staff member,
- suicide or homicide,
- substance overdose,
- death of classmate(s) or teacher,
- severe violence (e.g., gang fight),
- assault on a teacher or administrator,
- hostage situation on school grounds,
- child molestation,
- abandonment of a newborn in the school,
- sniper attack,
- terrorist activities,
- fire or chemical spill at school,
- plane, train, boat, bus or automobile accident, and
- natural disasters (e.g., tornado, flood, earthquake, etc.).

These events often impact large number of people and draw attention from the media. **However, it does not take a large-scale, highly publicized event to create marked disruption and dysfunction in a school.**

All traumatic experiences that adversely impact members of a school family may be viewed as crises. Consider the following:

- a student presents with bruises and reports that she was beaten by her parent
- a group of children were approached by a stranger in front of the school
- a high school student was found to be severely intoxicated
- a romantic relationship between two students suddenly terminated leaving one describing a suicidal plan
- a student was diagnosed with cancer
- teachers' purses were stolen from their classrooms
- a student's English essay was suggestive of a homicidal plan
- a fight erupted in the cafeteria
- the school was vandalized during the night
- a student was injured in the school playground during recess
- an altercation occurred between two staff members

How are schools responding to crises?

Due to the changing spirit of our times, school districts across the nation have been charged with the responsibility of developing comprehensive crisis response plans. These plans typically focus on the *structure* of crisis response—in the aftermath of a large-scale tragedy. For example, they address such issues as who will serve as members of a school crisis response team? What are the specific roles of team members? Who will gather the facts? How will team members be notified? What information will be shared with the school family? Who will address the media? etc.

Although structured plans have been developed and implemented by our school districts, little attention has been given to the *process* of school crisis response.

Although structured plans have been developed and implemented by our school districts, little attention has been given to the *process* of school crisis response. For example, once students have been assembled in a lounge, library, or other counseling venue, what is done to help them? What is the goal of early intervention? Who is truly prepared to address the emergent *psychological* needs of groups of people who are exhibiting emotional distress?

This edition of *A Practical Guide for Crisis Response in Our Schools* is a dramatically expanded publication that aims to provide a *structure* and *process* for effectively managing a wide spectrum of school-based crises—from the seemingly mundane to the most severe. No longer is school crisis response delegated solely to school administrators and members of a school crisis response team. Effective crisis management is the responsibility of *all* members of the school family.

No longer is school crisis response delegated solely to school administrators and members of a school crisis response team. Effective crisis management is the responsibility of *all* members of the school family.

This publication introduces and incorporates a practical and effective strategy for addressing the emotional needs of people *during* traumatic events, **Acute Traumatic Stress Management (ATSM)** (Lerner and Shelton, 2001). ATSM does not require caregivers to be mental health practitioners. Rather, **ATSM aims to empower all educators by providing a "road map" to keep people functioning and mitigate long-term emotional suffering. With effective school-based intervention, we can reestablish a productive educational process and prevent acute stress reactions from becoming chronic stress disorders.**

What is traumatic stress?

Traumatic stress refers to the emotional, cognitive, behavioral and physiological experience of individuals who are exposed to, or who witness, events that overwhelm their coping and problem-solving abilities. These events are often unexpected and uncontrollable. They compromise and individual's sense of safety and security and leave people feeling insecure and vulnerable. Traumatic stress disables people, causes disease, precipitates mental disorders, leads to substance abuse, and destroys relationships and families. **It is critical that our schools are prepared to respond to the wide range of traumatic events that can impact the school environment.**

Traumatic stress reactions can have a significant impact upon people and may ultimately lead to Posttraumatic Stress Disorder (PTSD). In these cases, individuals may experience recurrent and intrusive distressing recollections of the event, distressing dreams, flashbacks, difficulty concentrating, hypervigilance, an exaggerated startle response, and a host of avoidance behaviors. **Noteworthy is that children are much more likely to develop traumatic stress reactions and PTSD than are adults.**

Within the school setting, traumatic stress can impact both students *and* staff. Consider the following effects:

- a breakdown in communication between staff members
- a decrease in morale and group cohesiveness
- tension and conflict between students, as well as with staff members
- insubordination
- excessive absenteeism
- students earning failing grades
- workers' compensation, disability claims and litigation among staff members, and
- a marked disruption of the educational process.

Who experiences traumatic stress?

As indicated previously, traumatic stress is experienced by individuals who have been exposed to large-scale tragedies, as well as by individuals who experience day-to-day "personal tragedies." The following reflect the many "faces" of traumatic events that can significantly impact a school:

- a student was involved in a serious automobile accident

- a high school senior was assaulted by gang members

- a well-known athlete committed suicide

- a child reported that he was fondled by his baby-sitter

- students observed their social studies teacher collapse after suffering a heart attack

- a gun is found in a student's backpack

- a student describes an incident of domestic violence

Traumatic stress reactions may manifest themselves in the classroom, the cafeteria, the school bus, or the playground. Early identification and intervention may ultimately prevent undue disruption of the educational process and prevent debilitating stress disorders.

Is traumatic stress usually caused by "severe" events?

Generally, as the severity of a traumatic event increases, so does the level of traumatic stress. For example, if a student were to fall from the gymnasium bleachers and then lay on the floor clutching his ankle, one would expect the youngster, and those who observed the incident, to experience a degree of traumatic stress. However, if the boy lay on the ground apparently unconscious, bleeding heavily from his mouth, it is likely that the bystanders would experience a greater level of traumatic stress.

Events that are particularly gruesome, such as open wounds, will have a powerful impact upon those who witness the incident. Similarly, the sounds of children screaming and the smell of fire will leave a lasting impression. These perceptions collectively create what may be termed the "**Imprint of Horror**," and are often precipitators for posttraumatic stress reactions in the hours, days and months following the event.

Although the severity of the event may be one of the most important predictors of traumatic stress, it is important to recognize that *all* traumatic events have the potential to cause significant damage.

What factors influence how people respond to traumatic events?

The manner in which an individual responds to a traumatic event will be based upon many variables including **pre-trauma factors** (e.g., a history of emotional problems, learning disabilities, substance use, prior traumatic exposure, etc.), **characteristics of the traumatic event** (e.g., the severity, proximity, intentionally caused vs. natural disaster, etc.), and **post-trauma factors** (e.g., having the opportunity to "tell his story," level of familial support, etc.). These variables, in concert with individual characteristics and the "personal meaning" that an individual ascribes to a traumatic event, will ultimately determine how an individual will respond in the face of trauma.

What reactions do people exhibit *during* traumatic exposure?

In the same way that a high school biology teacher must have a strong understanding of human anatomy, botany and zoology, those who strive to help others who have been exposed to a traumatic event must have a strong understanding of how people react during traumatic exposure. The following emotional, cognitive, behavioral and physiological reactions are frequently observed. Not every response is evidenced by everyone, developmental factors will influence the response, and the order in which responses are exhibited will vary from person to person.

Emotional Responses may include shock, in which the individual may present a highly anxious, active response or perhaps a seemingly stunned, emotionally-numb response. He may describe feeling as though he is "in a fog." He may exhibit denial, in which there is an inability to acknowledge the impact of the situation or perhaps, that the situation has occurred. He may evidence dissociation, in which he may seem dazed and apathetic, and he may express feelings of unreality. Other frequently observed acute emotional responses may include panic, fear, intense feelings of aloneness, hopelessness, helplessness, emptiness, uncertainty, horror, terror, anger, hostility, irritability, depression, grief and feelings of guilt.

Cognitive Responses to traumatic exposure are often reflected in impaired concentration, confusion, disorientation, difficulty in making a decision, a short attention span, suggestibility, vulnerability, forgetfulness, self-blame, blaming others, lowered self-efficacy, thoughts of losing control, hypervigilance, and perseverative thoughts of the traumatic event. For example, after separating two students during a violent altercation, one of the students may cognitively still "be in" the fight "playing the tape" of the assault over and over in his mind.

Behavioral Responses in the face of a traumatic event may include withdrawal, "spacing-out," non-communication, changes in speech patterns, regressive behaviors, erratic movements, impulsivity, a reluctance to abandon property, seemingly aimless walking, pacing, an inability to sit still, an exaggerated startle response and antisocial behaviors.

Physiological Responses may include rapid heart beat, elevated blood pressure, difficulty breathing*, shock symptoms*, chest pains*, cardiac palpitations*, muscle tension and pains, fatigue, fainting, flushed face, pale appearance, chills, cold clammy skin, increased sweating, thirst, dizziness, vertigo, hyperventilation, headaches, grinding of teeth, twitches and gastrointestinal upset.

     * Require immediate medical evaluation

It is important to recognize that these emotional, cognitive, behavioral and physiological reactions do not necessarily represent an unhealthy or maladaptive response to a traumatic event. Rather, they may be viewed as normal responses to an abnormal event. When these reactions are experienced in the future (i.e., weeks, months or even years after the event), are joined by other symptoms (e.g., recurrent distressing dreams, "flashbacks," avoidance behaviors, etc.), and interfere with social, occupational or other important areas of functioning, a psychiatric disorder may be in evidence.

CHAPTER TWO
The School Crisis Response Team

School-based crises will not always necessitate the involvement of a team of professionals. For example, if a student reached-out to her teacher, after learning of the death of her grandparent, a team response may not be warranted. In this case, the teacher was approached by a student who trusted her and sought her guidance and support. The teacher, empowered with practical skills aimed at helping others during a traumatic event, may be highly effective in addressing this adolescent's needs. Perhaps a referral to a guidance counselor, school social worker or school psychologist will follow. However, events that impact a larger number of individuals may call for the collaborative efforts of a School Crisis Response Team.

Why establish a school-based Crisis Response Team (CRT)?

A CRT capitalizes on the fact that co-workers know each other, have communicated previously in some manner with one another, and can work collaboratively. If a building team is not feasible, then a district team comprised of members throughout the school district should be formed. **It is critical that schools capitalize on the collaborative relationships that exist among members of a school family.**

When should schools turn to "outside professionals?"

All **school personnel should be educated and empowered to effectively respond to school-based crises.** Many events can be managed by a well-trained staff member. As previously noted, other events will call for a team effort. When a crisis situation can be handled effectively by the school CRT, the school should remain sensitive to bringing-in professionals who may be perceived as "outsiders." The well-meaning efforts of "strangers with name tags" may be rebuffed and their presence may only exacerbate disorganization and confusion.

It is critical that local emergency services personnel (i.e., police, fire, emergency medical service) are knowledgeable about the unique characteristics of working with children, adolescents and adults within a school setting.

Some events will clearly tax and overwhelm a school district's ability to respond effectively (e.g., a mass casualty incident). Therefore, it is critical that local emergency services personnel (i.e., police, fire, emergency medical service) are knowledgeable about the unique characteristics of working with children, adolescents and adults within a school setting. The involvement of community mental health agencies may prove to be invaluable during such events.

Who should serve as members of a School Crisis Response Team?

Members of the School Crisis Response Team should include the following:

Principal

The principal maintains a critical position on the Crisis Response Team. He/She holds the most authority in the building and typically has responsibility for the actions taken by team members. The principal must obtain all available facts. This process often involves speaking with families as well as outside agencies (e.g., police department and/or local hospital). The principal functions as the liaison between the school building, the superintendent and other district administration. Additionally, he/she may be involved in addressing the media. Ideally, the principal is approachable and supportive, especially during times of crisis.

Assistant Principal/Dean

The assistant principal helps the principal by serving as a liaison between support personnel, students and the principal. He/She maintains primary authority in the absence of the principal. The assistant principal can prepare and arrange for the distribution of letters to be sent home to parents and guardians. Such letters can inform them of the facts surrounding the crisis and a summary of actions the school is taking to help students (see Practical Document K). The assistant principal can meet with parents/guardians as well as facilitate the referral process for outside support (perhaps, in conjunction with the psychologist and/or social worker). Finally, the assistant principal may serve as an alternate spokesperson for the media.

School Psychologist

School psychologists are in a position to facilitate the crisis response at several levels. By virtue of their training, they can educate school staff and students about what to expect—emotionally, cognitively, behaviorally and physically—as a result of exposure to a traumatic event (e.g., a suicide). School psychologists are trained to identify individuals who may be "at risk" or vulnerable to further psychological deterioration following exposure to a crisis situation. Additionally, they may provide coping strategies, follow-up counseling with individuals, and referrals to outside professionals when appropriate.

Social Worker

Social workers can work with school psychologists in maintaining the emotional well-being of individuals exposed to a crisis. They may conduct support groups (if indicated) and help in the identification of individuals in need of further assistance. Social workers may contact and work with parents of students to facilitate further support, perhaps, by a community mental health center, etc.

School Nurse

With his/her knowledge of physical problems, the nurse is in an ideal position to help students who are injured. Moreover, the nursing staff is typically trained to handle acute physical reactions to crisis exposure including hyperventilation, fainting, etc. The nurse may serve as a liaison between the local hospital and the school building. Nurses can document the nature of injuries and facilitate in the transport of individuals to the hospital (if necessary).

Guidance Counselor

By virtue of their relationships with many students, guidance counselors may aid in identifying those individuals who are in need of intervention. They can coordinate support groups for students and staff, provide counseling as well as notify parents and guardians of students affected by the crisis (if indicated).

Teachers

Teachers may have the difficult task of providing a stable and calm model for their students at a time when they, personally, may be experiencing considerable emotional turmoil. A careful selection of teachers should be included on the Crisis Response Team. These teachers can serve as a liaison between the team and the faculty. Moreover, these teachers may be in a position to answer questions that students have regarding the crisis situation (assuming that by doing so, the emotional well-being of the student is prioritized). Teachers can help identify and refer students who appear in need of emotional support. Specific guidelines for teachers are offered in Practical Document C.

Building Security

Some schools have security guards on campus. Security guards maintain an important role in safeguarding individuals in the building in the event of a violent or potentially life-threatening situation. Building security should maintain direct contact and work in concert with local police (if indicated). Security guards can engage in crowd control in the event bystanders gather in the wake of an event. School classrooms, halls, cafeterias and grounds may need special monitoring.

Ancillary Staff

Other building staff may serve important roles during a crisis situation. For example, secretaries likely know many parents and students, and may supply the Crisis Response Team with relevant information. They may also be helpful in documentation. In addition, paraprofessionals (e.g., teacher aides) frequently have close relationships with many students within the school environment. These relationships could be invaluable in reaching students during a crisis. Finally, it is important that all staff, including non-teaching staff (e.g., custodians), have basic knowledge of the school's crisis response plan.

Other Team Members

Depending upon the nature and scope of a traumatic event, schools may need to call upon the resources of other individuals and organizations. Therefore, consideration should be given to involving other individuals as members of the school-based CRT. For example, the President of the PTA, a representative from local police, fire or rescue, the school district's director of buildings and grounds, the director of a community mental health agency, etc.

CHAPTER THREE

The Crisis Response Team in Action

Crisis situations often render those involved feeling confused, overwhelmed and helpless. Upon recognition of a significant traumatic event, the school Crisis Response Team moves into action. An efficient response plan makes both the physical and emotional safety of individuals a priority; this includes students, teachers, administrators, support and ancillary staff. It is always important to *think before acting*.

As described previously, traumatic events cause a host of emotional, cognitive, behavioral and physiological reactions. **In an effort to protect and help students, faculty and staff should keep in mind that the acute phase of the crisis is *not going to last forever*.** Carefully assess each step of the plan *before* it is enacted. Practical Document A is a Crisis Response Checklist which can serve as an invaluable resource *during* a crisis.

Although crisis response plans may vary from school district to school district, as will the availability of staff, a comprehensive crisis response plan should consider the following intervention strategies upon recognition of a crisis situation.

I. Fact Gathering

The first person to become aware of a crisis should contact the principal who will then notify school district administration. The primary task for the principal at this point is the gathering of details surrounding the crisis event. In the event of a fatal accident or suicide, this may involve making contact with the parents/guardians of the student(s).

Contacting parents/guardians after such tragic loss is an uncomfortable but necessary task. For example, when calling the parents of a child fatally injured in a motor vehicle accident, it may be important to ascertain:

- the events surrounding the youngster's death,
- how much information the parents want disclosed to the school community,
- whether funeral arrangements have been made,
- whether the parents approve of students and faculty attending the funeral, and
- if there is anything that the school can do for the family during this difficult time.

In the event of a devastating fire or natural disaster, contact with the fire department, police department, and/or local hospital is necessary for clarification of the facts surrounding the crisis.

It is also important that the principal keep in mind that people who are involved in a crisis situation are typically quite distressed and disoriented and consequently, information about the event(s) may be difficult to obtain. School personnel must be careful when inquiring about the sequence of events surrounding a crisis situation. For example, simple questions may be perceived as an interrogation and as invasive to those who witnessed a tragic event.

Rumors may abound and, at times, exacerbate chaos and confusion. It is important that personnel avoid assumptions about the nature of a crisis. For example, unless an official determination has been made for a cause of death, it is inappropriate to assume and label the cause of death as "suicide" even if it is quite obvious (Sandoval & Brock, 1996).

The principal should meet with the assistant principal and/or the school psychologist and determine the appropriateness of assembling the Crisis Response Team. Some of the variables to consider should include, but not be limited to, the **severity** of the event, the **number** of individuals affected by the event and the **reactions** of the students and faculty. Some situations may not require a crisis team intervention. For example, if the parent of a student was killed in an accident, contact with that student, his/her close friends, and teachers who knew the family may be more appropriate. In-school counseling and support should be offered to the individuals affected by the tragedy. If necessary, referrals for outside resources should also be provided. This may include specific professionals (e.g., psychologists), local mental health agencies, support groups (e.g., bereavement groups), and/or clergy.

If, upon consultation, it is decided that the Crisis Response Team is needed, then members are immediately notified. During school hours, the school should have a signal system that will communicate a message to the Crisis Response Team that they are being summoned. For example, the principal can make a public address announcement such as, "Will the principal's discussion team please report to the faculty lounge?" This signal will indicate that the Crisis Response Team is meeting immediately at that time.

An Emergency Contact List can be utilized if the crisis occurs during out-of-school hours (see Practical Document G). If the crisis occurs on a weekend, an announcement should be made on the next school day (see Practical Document H).

II. The Call to Action

Once the Crisis Response Team is assembled, it is critical that the team maintains a "pulse" on student and faculty reactions to the event. An attempt to estimate the size of the impact on the school community must be made. Things to consider should include:

- When did the event occur (e.g., during a lunch period, over the summer)?
- Where did the event occur (e.g., on school grounds)?
- How did it happen (e.g., accidental, intentional, expected)?
- How many students and staff were affected by the event?
- Which students and staff were affected?
- How were the students and staff affected?
- How are the faculty responding?
- Should classes be suspended temporarily or assignments altered?
- Should students be released from school?
- How are students indirectly being affected (e.g., siblings/ friends at other buildings in the school district, etc.)?

The school district administration (e.g., superintendent) should continually be updated as the crisis develops. A determination to seek additional support resources (e.g., personnel from other school district buildings and/or outside community) should be made and acted upon. A local community counseling center may be able to offer counseling support if needed. It may be helpful for outside professionals to wear an identification badge. School personnel and students need to be acquainted with unfamiliar faces. Finally, the principal/assistant principal should determine if substitute teachers are needed.

III. Notification Procedures

Depending upon the nature of the incident, the Crisis Response Team must determine how the students, faculty, and staff will be notified of the crisis. Some methods to consider should include:

- an **announcement** to students and faculty,
- a student **assembly**,
- a mailbox **memorandum** to faculty and staff,
- an emergency faculty **meeting** (first thing in the morning), and
- notification to students in **classrooms** by the Crisis Response Team.

Typically, the building principal will make the announcement to the students and faculty early in the day (see sample announcement, Practical Document H). He or she should state whatever facts are known about the incident in order to help prevent and/or dispel rumors. **It is important that consent (e.g., from a victim's guardian) has been granted prior to release of sensitive information.** Announcements should be simple and void of details that could be easily misinterpreted. In the case of a student suicide or death, medical details and specific circumstances should be avoided. A straightforward announcement that conveys sympathy and a statement of condolence is recommended. The principal's statement should convey the following to the school community:

- facts regarding the event,
- the location of assemblies (if applicable),
- the location of support personnel (e.g., psychologist, social worker, guidance counselors),
- resources to utilize outside of school hours, and
- the need for students to sign *out* of their assigned class and *in* at designated counseling areas (i.e., for secondary level students).

In the case of a suicide, it is important that the statement is void of glorification and/or condoning of the act. Moreover, if a student assembly is chosen as a means to announce the crisis, then it is important to consider that a primary goal is to *efficiently* serve large numbers of students.

Weinberg (1990) has suggested that additional objectives of an *assembly* should be to:

- describe and normalize healthy grief reactions,
- observe students' and staff reactions—to identify individuals who are in need of further support (e.g., counseling), and
- encourage adaptive coping strategies and discourage unhealthy, maladaptive ones.

When deciding on the mode of communication about the crisis situation with the students (i.e., public address, assembly, etc.), the Crisis Response Team should consider:

- the **nature** of the crisis situation (e.g., accidental, suicide, etc.),
- the **age** of the students,
- the availability of **support services** (within and outside of the school) and,
- the needs and concerns of **parents/guardians** of the students.

As indicated previously, *confidentiality* must remain a top priority during times of crisis. In some circumstances, for example in the death of a student, the parents of that student should be contacted by the principal and consent should be granted before an official announcement is made to the school community. Information regarding funeral arrangements (if applicable) may be shared upon consent of the family (see sample memorandum to the faculty, Practical Document J).

Some administrators find that commencing (and possibly concluding) the school day with an emergency faculty meeting serves as a helpful adjunct to the circulation of a memo. Additionally, it is a more personal way to address a traumatic event such as a student's (or faculty member's) death. The principal should address the concerns of the faculty and staff, receive feedback from them and answer their questions. It could be helpful for a Crisis Response Team member to review warning signs (e.g., appearing detached, confused, disoriented, agitated, anxious, depressed, etc.) for high risk students and differences between age-appropriate responses and maladaptive reactions (see Chapter 5). This will aid the faculty in identifying students (and/or colleagues) in need of further support.

Depending upon the circumstances, the principal may suggest to teachers that they begin their classes by discussing the event and give students an opportunity to express themselves and their concerns. In all likelihood, upon notification of distressing news (e.g., death of a peer), concentration, interest and motivation for instruction will be significantly impaired. The postponement of tests should be considered.

The responses of the faculty should be monitored. When the crisis involves the death of a student, it is important to consider that many staff members develop close relationships with students and their reactions must not be overlooked. All individuals in the school building should be informed that staff (e.g., psychologist, social worker, and/or guidance counselors) are available for them at this difficult time. The locations and availability of support personnel should be posted in a highly visible and accessible area and confidentiality should be assured. Follow-up faculty and staff meetings should be planned (if indicated).

IV. Crisis Response Team in Motion

Administrators and/or security may circulate in the building to be available for, and perhaps refer, students or staff for support. The building principal may need to remove personal items from a student's desk or locker to save for parents and family (Petersen & Straub, 1992). The principal and/or district administration should prepare a letter to be sent home to parents (see sample letter, Practical Document K).

Letters to parents should state:

- the facts surrounding the crisis,

- a summary of actions the school is taking to help students,

- a list of reactions to expect from their child,

- guidelines that can aid the parent(s) in providing support to their child(ren), and

- contact phone numbers within and/or outside of the school for further information and support.

Building security should maintain direct contact and collaborate with the local police and/or the fire department (if indicated). Security guards can engage in crowd control in the event bystanders gather in the wake of an event. School classrooms, halls, cafeterias and grounds may need special monitoring.

> **It may be helpful for Crisis Response Team members to view themselves as consultants to teachers—providing information and intervention on an as-needed basis.**

Within the classroom, teachers should allow opportunity for students to acknowledge and discuss their thoughts and feelings associated with the crisis. By validating their students' feelings, teachers can facilitate the grieving process. Teachers should reinforce that it could be very helpful to talk with support personnel regarding their feelings about the incident. It is important that other members of the Crisis Response Team are sensitive to a teacher's beliefs concerning the type and amount of intervention that is provided in his/her classroom. It may be helpful for Crisis Response Team members to view themselves as consultants to teachers—providing information and intervention on an as-needed basis. A detailed description of what classroom teachers can do to address the reactions of their students to a crisis situation can be found in Practical Document C. Finally, the locations of support staff should be made available in a clear manner and should be posted in a highly visible place for students and staff.

Individual and small group counseling (e.g., preferably between five and eight students) provided by school psychologists, social workers and guidance counselors can offer an appropriate forum for students to express themselves (Davidson, 1989). All personnel who counsel individuals in crisis should keep in mind that:

- Listening to others in a non-judgmental, warm and genuine manner is an important goal.

- All individuals have the right to their own opinions and feelings.

- Making effective contact with another individual involves establishing rapport.

- Lecturing, preaching and/or criticizing are barriers to effective communication.

- Cultural differences exist in the overt expression of emotions.

- Maintaining confidentiality, when possible, is crucial.

- It is important to remember that *you* have support while helping others during a crisis situation.

Rooms accessible to all students, faculty and staff should be designated, especially for the purpose of counseling. This space should be continually staffed with members of the Crisis Response Team. Given the great potential for crisis counseling to become stressful for support personnel over time, a rotation of members is highly recommended.

The principal (or assistant principal) can arrange for snacks (e.g., juice, cookies, etc.) to be provided to students and support personnel. This type of accommodation often gives students a sense of comfort at such a difficult time. Teachers should be notified when their students are absent from their class (minimal information should be disclosed). It is common during times of crisis for staff members to neglect eating meals and/or to work incessantly at helping others; in the process, fatigue and exhaustion are exacerbated by lack of nutrition—caretakers must also take care of themselves.

It is essential that individuals of all ages exposed to a traumatic event have an opportunity to ventilate, to "tell their story," and feel supported by those around them. Additionally, it is important that an educational component exists in the intervention process. For example, student's who have been involved in a school bus accident need to know that they may likely experience frequent recollections of the event—like "playing a videotape over an over in your mind." They should be informed that it is not unusual to experience difficulty sleeping, eating and concentrating and that they may experience headaches or feelings of nausea. This educational component helps to normalize responses to an abnormal situation, and helps survivors to know that they are not alone and that they are not "going crazy." Age-appropriate reactions and specific intervention strategies are addressed in Chapter 5.

Additionally, psychologists and social workers may work with high risk students and involve parents if deemed necessary. High risk students (e.g., suicidal) may include those:

- who were close with the victim(s),

- who have experienced prior tragedy (e.g., death in family),

- known to engage in substance abuse,

- who are depressed,

- who describe their situation as "hopeless,"

- who are experiencing sleep and/or eating disturbances,

- who talk about "not being around...,"
- who give-away possessions,
- who articulate a suicide plan, and those
- with a history of self-destructive behaviors, etc.

Referrals to appropriate outside professionals, including local community mental health clinics, hospitals and practitioners must occur if a student (or staff member) is injured, in shock, or presents with seriously adverse emotional and/or behavioral reactions (e.g., suicidal ideation and/or intent). In the event of refusal by a parent or guardian to heed the school district's recommendations for outside intervention for a student clearly in need of assistance, referral to the local child protection agency must be considered. Moreover, hot line information and phone numbers for community mental health clinics should be provided to all students and faculty for contact (if needed) after regular school hours.

Careful documentation of all students counseled and efforts to intervene is crucial. A detailed log should be kept because it could help in the treatment of these individuals upon referral to an outside resource. Documentation of the course of events is also necessary for proper in-school follow-up after the crisis situation has been resolved.

> **Members of the Crisis Response Team must always remain sensitive to how others are perceiving them. If their mood is incongruent with the general climatic mood, they will likely be perceived as lacking genuineness and may be rebuffed by the very individuals who most need their services.**

A forum at the school, for parents to discuss and receive support on managing the effects of the crisis on their child at school and home, should be considered (e.g., in the evening). Members of the Crisis Response Team could offer important insight at such a meeting.

On the days following the crisis, the availability of support personnel is crucial. Students and faculty should be reminded that support staff, such as the psychologist, social worker and/or guidance counselors, are available for continued help if they feel a need to talk. Oftentimes, the emotional impact of a crisis situation is experienced weeks and, perhaps, months after the event has resolved. The school district should maintain a follow-up plan to ensure that individuals affected by the crisis receive proper support and intervention. Follow-up faculty meetings can address concerns of the staff and faculty as they arise.

Members of the Crisis Response Team must always remain sensitive to how others are perceiving them. If their mood is incongruent with the general climatic mood, they will likely be perceived as lacking genuineness and may be rebuffed by the very individuals who most need their services. For example, it would not be advisable for a team member to engage in a general social conversation about extraneous issues in full view of the "victims."

V. Addressing the Media

Depending upon the nature of the crisis, a plan to deal with the media should be considered. Crisis situations, especially in the school system, tend to precipitate the interest of news stations. Knowledge of what and how much information to share with the media should be determined by administration—perhaps in consultation with the Crisis Response Team (see sample announcement to the media, Practical Document I). Factors to consider include:

- the confidentiality of those involved in the crisis,
- the wishes of the family members of victims, and
- the potential liability and confusion that could result from dissemination of erroneous information.

An individual (e.g., superintendent, building principal) should be selected in preparation for media coverage. It is strongly recommended that other personnel be discouraged from disclosing information to the media unless permission is granted from their direct supervisors (e.g., principal). An alternate spokesperson, knowledgeable about the facts surrounding the crisis event, should be selected in the event that the designated speaker becomes unavailable for the media.

VI. Debriefing

The Crisis Response Team should reconvene before leaving the school. This debriefing period is a necessary part of any comprehensive crisis intervention plan (Sandoval & Brock, 1996). The debriefing permits a review of the precipitating events that may have led to the crisis situation and the manner in which the Crisis Response Team has managed the circumstances. Follow-up actions are reviewed and personnel may be selected to contact students and their families who were most significantly affected by the event. Assuming proper consent is granted, follow-up contact with outside referral sources, such as mental health professionals, may be helpful.

The emotional reactions and thoughts of the Crisis Response Team should be addressed during the debriefing period as well. Caregivers are not immune to the traumatization that often occurs in the wake of a tragic event. Figley (1995) has described "compassion fatigue" as a potential consequence of working with individuals in crisis. In their effort to protect, assist, and heal, helpers pay a cost—emotionally, cognitively and behaviorally—and can develop posttraumatic symptoms as a result of their exposure to these events. It may be beneficial for the psychologist to provide materials to the Crisis Response Team on stress and its management as well as information on trauma and its effects on individuals (see Traumatic Stress: An Overview, Practical Document M). If necessary, the appropriate referrals should be made to support staff.

VII. Funerals

In the event of the death of a student, attendance at the victim's funeral is a decision that should be made by all students' families. Additionally, the wishes of the family of the deceased should always be considered when individuals desire to attend or take part in the funeral. Assuming that consent is granted by family members, attendance at the funeral service may facilitate closure to very difficult and confusing circumstances. Members of the Crisis Response Team should be available to students before and after funeral services. If possible, school support personnel should accompany students to the funeral services. The age of the individual is of utmost priority in determining funeral attendance. The concept of death is vague and abstract for many elementary students and careful discretion is therefore advised.

VIII. Memorialization

It has been suggested that following a crisis event, some form of memorialization may facilitate the grieving process (Sandoval & Brock, 1996). This can take the form of a moment of silence, a plaque, planting a tree, a dedication, flying the flag at half-mast, etc. Some researchers have suggested that memorials may serve to glorify and reinforce the attention that death or tragic loss brings and should be avoided altogether (McKee, Jones, & Richardson, 1991). Ideally, the decision to establish a memorial should be made with special consideration given to the nature of the crisis (e.g., accidental death, suicide), needs of the students involved (including their age), and consensus of the school district administration.

CHAPTER FOUR

Acute Traumatic Stress Management for Educators

A wide spectrum of traumatic events can impact a school. Some events will likely call upon the efforts of a school Crisis Response Team (e.g., a student suicide). Other events can be effectively addressed by individuals who are committed to helping others in times of crisis (e.g., the death of a grandparent). This chapter offers practical skills to empower *all* educators. It offers a strategy, a "road map" to guide individuals through times of crisis, to keep people functioning and to mitigate long-term emotional suffering.

During times of crisis, we are quick to address physical and safety needs. Depending upon the nature of the event, school administrators scramble, the school nurse is summoned and building security is alerted. Other crises may call primarily for the trained ear and empathic heart of a teacher or counselor. Much has been written about post-crisis intervention, "psychological first-aid" introduced in the aftermath of a tragedy. In recent years, effective interventions have been developed to address the emotional needs of people after disengagement from a crisis—following a traumatic experience. For example, schools have called-upon teams of counselors to "debrief" students and staff. Notwithstanding, there is little information for educators offering practical strategies to help people *during* a traumatic event. This is a time when individuals are perhaps most suggestible and vulnerable to traumatic stress, a tremendous opportunity for intervention.

During times of crisis, we experience the "Imprint of Horror," the sights, sounds and/or smells that are recorded in our minds. Consider a school bus accident, a gang fight in the cafeteria, or images of a beloved teacher collapsing in front of his students. These perceptions may be the precipitators of acute traumatic stress reactions and chronic stress disorders. **In the same way that these negative stimuli are etched in our minds during traumatic exposure, a time of heightened suggestibility and vulnerability, so too can a positive, adaptive force—***Acute Traumatic Stress Management*** (Lerner and Shelton, 2001).

Acute Traumatic Stress Management (ATSM) is a practical approach to address the emergent psychological needs of people *during* traumatic events. It provides caregivers with "practical tools" for addressing the spectrum of traumatic experiences—from mild to the most severe. It is a goal-directed process delivered within the framework of a facilitative or helping attitudinal climate. ATSM aims to "jump-start" an individual's coping and problem-solving abilities. It seeks to stabilize acute symptoms of traumatic stress and stimulate healthy, adaptive functioning. Finally, ATSM may increase the likelihood of an individual pursuing mental health intervention, if need be, in the future. ATSM is *not* a comprehensive crisis intervention or disaster response plan and does not require advanced training or a degree in mental health. Rather, ATSM may be viewed as a practical strategy to complement an educators' repertoire of helping skills (Lerner and Shelton, 2001).

ATSM was orginally developed for emergency responders, not educators. Though one may point out that the changing spirit of our times has blurred the line between the two. ATSM is implemented through 10 stages that offer a degree of structure during a typically unstructured period of time:

1. Assess for Danger/Safety for Self and Others
2. Consider the Mechanism of Injury
3. Evaluate the Level of Responsiveness
4. Address Medical Needs
5. Observe and Identify
6. Connect with the Individual
7. Ground the Individual
8. Provide Support
9. Normalize the Response
10. Prepare for the Future

Following is a discussion of the stages of ATSM. The first five stages are of primary importance to "first responders" and have to do with considerations surrounding situation management and emergency medical care. Within the school environment, these initial stages may be most appropriately implemented by school administrators, security personnel, the school nurse, school psychologist and social worker. During events that tax or overwhelm a school's ability to respond effectively (e.g., a fire, shooting, building collapse, etc.), these stages may very well be addressed by fire, police and EMS personnel. The latter five stages may be implemented by all caregivers.

It is important to recognize that the nature of the event, as well as the intensity of individuals' reactions, will vary during traumatic exposure. Consequently, appropriate intervention may not fall neatly into a linear progression of stages. Thus, you will need to be flexible given the presenting circumstances.

1. Assess for Danger/Safety for Self and Others

Upon arrival at the scene of a traumatic event, assess the situation in order to determine whether there are factors that can compromise your safety or the safety of others. You will be of little help to someone else if you are injured. For example, avoid placing yourself in the middle of fighting adolescents without the presence of other staff members. Depending upon the nature of the event, it may be necessary to approach with school security or call for police intervention. During traumatic events, remove the individual(s) from a location, or from other individuals, rather than risk further traumatic exposure.

2. Consider the Mechanism of Injury

Form an initial impression of those impacted by the event. In order to understand the nature of an individual's *exposure*, **it is important to assess how the event may have physically impacted the individual—that is, how environmental factors transferred to the person.** For example, if a student is found lying unconscious on the gymnasium floor next to open bleachers, it is important to determine where the student fell from. How high up was he? What part of his body struck the floor? Did his head have contact with the bleacher prior to hitting the floor? etc. **It is also important to consider the** *perceptual* **experiences of victims.** For example, observing a teacher collapse and suffer a fatal heart attack will have a powerful impact on those who directly observed the incident. Similarly, the sounds of students screaming following a stabbing in the school cafeteria will etch a lasting impression in peoples' psyches (i.e., the "Imprint of Horror").

3. Evaluate the Level of Responsiveness

It is important to determine if an individual is alert and responsive to verbal stimuli. Does he feel pain? Is he aware of what has occurred, or what is presently occurring? Is he under the influence of a substance? During a traumatic event it is quite possible that the individual is experiencing "emotional" shock. Therefore, symptomatology may mimic acute medical conditions (i.e., rapid changes in respiration, pulse, blood pressure, etc.). Recognize that a psychological state of shock may be adaptive in preventing the individual from experiencing the full impact of the event too quickly. In the case of a 14 year-old boy who was informed that his grandfather had suddenly passed-away, he stared blankly at his guidance counselor and initially did not respond. His reaction was not unusual. **During traumatic events, people may experience a wide range of emotional reactivity.**

During traumatic events, people may experience a wide range of emotional reactivity.

4. Address Medical Needs

Within the school environment, the school nurse is charged with the responsibility of addressing emergent medical needs. It is critical that medical intervention is only provided by trained healthcare professionals. It is also imperative that EMS personnel are contacted quickly in the event of a serious illness or injury. Consider the potential danger of moving the youngster, described previously, who had fallen from the bleachers. Despite the best intentions of a staff member, the youngster could have suffered a serious back injury and movement could cause permanent injury to his spinal cord. **It is imperative that life-threatening illness and injury are always addressed prior to psychological needs.**

5. Observe and Identify

Observe and identify those who have been exposed to the traumatic event. Very often, these individuals will not be the direct victims. They may be "secondary" or "hidden victims." Remember, witnessing or even being exposed to another individual who has faced traumatic exposure can cause traumatic stress. As you observe and identify who has been exposed to the event (i.e., directly and/or indirectly), begin to observe and identify who is evidencing signs of traumatic stress. An awareness of the emotional, cognitive, behavioral and physiological reactions suggestive of traumatic stress is important (see Chapter 1). Carefully look around you. Anyone, including yourself, may be a direct or hidden victim. Consider the following story:

> Following the suicide of a high school senior, school administrators encouraged friends of the deceased adolescent to sign out of class and go to the school library for support. School psychologists, social workers and counselors were on hand. A freshman student entered the library, signed-in and took a seat near the door. A number of students began talking about the freshman—"He wasn't a friend of Bobby..... He didn't even know him...." Talk quickly turned to anger— "Some people around here are just looking for a reason to get out of class. They didn't give a — about Bobby!" A school psychologist observed the freshman who seemed detached and "lost." He then spoke individually with the boy. The youngster, Steven, acknowledged that he did not know Bobby. However, Steven shared with the psychologist that *he* was seriously contemplating suicide and that he wanted to know, "What happens after someone kills himself?" Steven was subsequently evaluated by a psychiatrist and hospitalized for several weeks for severe depression.

This story certainly reflects the feelings of anger that may be manifested during a crisis. Additionally, it underscores the importance in looking beyond those individuals who are perceived as the "direct" victims of a tragedy.

6. Connect with the Individual

During a crisis, introduce yourself and let people know *your* role in the school. If the individual is not physically injured or has been seen by the school nurse or cleared by other emergency medical personnel, move him away to prevent further traumatic exposure. Begin to develop rapport by making an effort to understand

and appreciate his situation. A simple question such as, "How are you doing?" may be used to engage the individual. Use appropriate non-verbal communication (e.g., eye contact, body turned toward him, a gentle touch, etc.). **Recognize that during traumatic events, individual reactions may present on a continuum from a totally detached, withdrawn reaction to the most intense displays of emotion (e.g., uncontrollable crying, screaming, panic, anger, fear, etc.).**

7. Ground the Individual

When you have established a connection with someone who has been exposed to a traumatic event (e.g., eye contact, body turned toward you, dialogue directed at you, etc.), you can initiate this grounding stage. Begin by acknowledging the traumatic event at a factual level. **Here, you attempt to orient the individual by discussing the *facts* surrounding the event. Address the circumstances of the event at a cognitive, or thinking level. While we do not discourage the expression of emotion, attempt to focus on the facts in the here-and-now, and help the individual to know the reality of the situation.** Oftentimes, his "reality" may be seriously clouded due to the nature of the event. Remember, traumatic events overwhelm an individual's usual coping and problem-solving abilities. Assure the individual that he is now safe, if he is. **He may still be "playing the tape" of the traumatic event over and over in his head. By reviewing facts, you may disrupt "negative cognitive rehearsal" and help the individual to begin to deal with the actual circumstances at hand.**

> While we do not discourage the expression of emotion, attempt to focus on the facts in the here-and-now, and help the individual to know the reality of the situation.

> Following a serious injury of a young football player, team members were unable to stop thinking about the play-gone-wrong. They described how their teammate jumped to grab the ball and was hit from behind. The boys described how they couldn't "stop the tape" in their minds. They were repeatedly visualizing their teammate landing on his head and even hearing the sound of his body thumping on the ground.

It is important to "place the individual in the situation." Encourage him to "tell his story" and describe where he was, what he saw, what it sounded like, what it smelled like, what he did, and how his body responded. Encourage the individual to discuss his behavioral and physiological response to the event —rather than "how it felt."

8. Provide Support

Factual discussion and the realization of a traumatic event, particularly when the event is still occurring, may likely stimulate thoughts and feelings. This is often the time when individuals who are exposed to trauma need the most support. However, in reality, it is also the time when many people look the other way. Many individuals feel terribly unprepared to handle others' painful thoughts and feelings. Oftentimes, they fear that they will "open a can of worms" or "say the wrong thing."

It is important to establish and maintain a *facilitative* **or** *helping attitudinal climate.* **Here, you attempt to understand and respect the uniqueness of the individual—the thoughts and feelings that he is experiencing. You strive to "give back" a sense of control that has been "taken from" him by virtue of his exposure to the event. You support him, and you allow him to think and feel. In the face of traumatic exposure, many people experience an overwhelming sense of aloneness and withdraw into their own world. You should make a respectful** effort to "enter that world," and to help the individual to know that he is not alone and that his unique perception of his experience is important. Do not attempt to talk a person out of a feeling (e.g., "Don't be scared, you're fine."). Communicate an appreciation of the other person's experience. Attempt to understand the feelings that lie behind his words (or perhaps actions) and convey that understanding to him.

> In the face of traumatic exposure, many people experience an overwhelming sense of aloneness and withdraw into their own world. You should make a respectful effort to "enter that world," and to help the individual to know that he is not alone and that his unique perception of his experience is important.

9. Normalize the Response

While you are attempting to support an individual by giving him the opportunity to express his thoughts and feelings, begin to normalize his reaction to the traumatic event. This is an important component when intervening with people who have been exposed to trauma and who may be feeling very alone. Experiencing a cascade of emotions or perhaps a lack of emotional expression, may cause him to feel as if he is "losing it" and perhaps, "going crazy." **Normalizing and validating an individual's experience will help him to know that he is a** *normal* **person trying to deal with an** *abnormal* **event.**

It is important that you do not become sympathetic and overidentify with the situation with statements such as, "I know what it feels like... when I was in high school...." Rather, you should attempt to normalize and validate the individual's experience with statements like, "I see this is overwhelming for you right now... seeing your classmate seriously hurt would be hard for anyone to handle."

An important component of the normalization process is to begin to *educate* the individual by helping him to know how people typically respond to traumatic events. Refer to the emotional, cognitive, behavioral and physiological responses outlined in Chapter 1. Remember that these reactions do not necessarily represent an unhealthy or maladaptive response. Rather, they may be viewed as normal responses to an abnormal event. When these reactions are experienced in the future (i.e., weeks, months or even years after the event), are joined by other symptoms (e.g., recurrent distressing dreams, "flashbacks," avoidance behaviors, etc.), and interfere with social, occupational or other important areas of functioning, a psychiatric disorder may be in evidence. These individuals should pursue help with a mental health professional.

An important component of the normalization process is to begin to *educate* the individual by helping him to know how people typically respond to traumatic events.

10. Prepare for the Future

The final phase of the ATSM process is aimed at preparing the individual for what lies on the road ahead. **It is helpful to, 1) review the nature of the traumatic event, 2) bring the person to the present, and 3) describe likely events in the future.** The educational process initiated during the previous normalization stage should continue during this final stage of ATSM.

Be careful not to tell someone as you near the end of your intervention that "everything is going to be okay" or that "everything is going to work out." These kinds of "band-aid" statements may only serve to minimize an individual's feelings and cause him to feel misunderstood. Instead, focus on the facilitative attitudinal climate that you have established—"I'm glad that I had the opportunity to be here with you during such a difficult time."

Conclusion

Acute Traumatic Stress Management offers educators a practical strategy for addressing the emotional needs of students and staff *during* traumatic events. Recognize that ATSM should not be viewed as counseling or psychotherapy and that, in and of itself, ATSM is not a comprehensive school crisis response plan. Rather, ATSM offers a "road map" to guide individuals through times of crisis, to keep people functioning and mitigate long-term emotional suffering.

CHAPTER FIVE

Age-Appropriate Reactions & Specific Intervention Strategies

The manner in which people react to crisis situations is dependent upon a number of variables including personal history, personality variables, severity and proximity of the event, level of social support and the type and quality of intervention. While no two people respond to situations, including crisis situations, in exactly the same manner, the following are often seen as early reactions to a crisis (age-appropriate reactions, as well as age-specific interventions, will be addressed shortly):

- shock—numbness,

- denial or inability to acknowledge the situation has occurred,

- dissociative behavior—appearing dazed, apathetic, expressing feelings of unreality,

- confusion,

- disorganization,

- difficulty making a decision, and

- suggestibility.

The following information will be particularly helpful in your work with individuals of different ages. This information, utilized within the framework of the **Acute Traumatic Stress Management** model (see Chapter 4), offers practical tools to understand and help individuals who have been exposed to traumatic events.

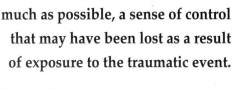

It is important to give back, as much as possible, a sense of control that may have been lost as a result of exposure to the traumatic event.

An important objective of school crisis response is to develop rapport. Empathy, warmth and genuineness are crucial in leading to understanding and trust and ultimately, to disclosure of thoughts and feelings (Lerner, 1988). It is important to give back, as much as possible, a sense of control that may have been lost as a result of exposure to the traumatic event. Educators must recognize trust issues, particularly when individuals have been violated. For example, a child who has been molested by an adult may have difficulty sharing thoughts or feelings about the experience with another adult. Similarly, a high school girl who has been raped may find it difficult speaking with a male counselor about the experience.

As described previously (see Chapter 4) **it is crucial to provide individuals who have been exposed to traumatic events an opportunity to "tell their story." The goal here is not so much aimed at helping the victim to "feel better" as much as to prevent a maladaptive response.** This is a critical point. Too frequently caregivers misinterpret denial experienced by the victim as a sense of coping. This seeming adaptation is dangerous because it may lead to reinforcement of further denial or worse, "running from" intervention. Finally, it is important not to be confrontational during early crisis response.

While individuals are being provided with an opportunity to articulate their thoughts and feelings in a warm and supportive climate, as well as educated about some of the common responses to traumatic events (see age-appropriate reactions which follow), it may be helpful to:

- Talk about the facts surrounding the experience
- Talk about behaviors at the time of the experience (e.g., Where exactly were you and what were you doing?)
- Talk about physical reactions at the time of the experience (e.g., How did your body respond?)
- Talk about thoughts at the time and immediately after the experience (e.g., What was going through your mind?)
- Talk about feelings at the time and immediately after the experience (e.g., What were you feeling?)

Finally, it may be helpful to ask, "What was the worst thing about the experience for you?" One should expect considerable variability from person to person and be careful not to judge their response. **Again, it is crucial to give back a sense of control and help to empower individuals.**

Understanding the typical reactions of individuals exposed to a crisis situation is a critical step in identifying people who may be in need of further professional assistance. Several investigators (Greenstone & Levittown, 1993; Klingman, 1987; Pitcher & Poland, 1992; Weaver, 1995) have described age-appropriate reactions of individuals exposed to a traumatic event. Although there is heterogeneity in the reactions of individuals surrounding a crisis, most of these responses are expected reactions and subside in several weeks following the crisis. A list of possible interventions is included within each age category.

Preschool Children (Ages 1 through 5)

Engaging in behaviors that are immature and that have been abandoned in the past including:

- thumb sucking
- bed wetting
- fear of the dark
- loss of bladder control
- speech difficulties
- decreases or increases in appetite
- clinging and whining
- separation difficulties

Interventions:

Preschool children do not yet possess the cognitive skills to understand a crisis and lack the coping strategies to deal with it effectively. They therefore look to adults in their environment for support and comfort. Preschool childrens' reactions to a crisis are governed by how significant adults react. They are vulnerable to sudden changes and/or disruptions in their environment which frequently results in them viewing their world as "unsafe" and "scary." The young child's main concern during a crisis will likely be if they are going to be abandoned. Interventions need to focus on offering support and reassurance, while at the same time helping the child to express his/her feelings. Because younger children typically do not have this ability to adequately express their feelings, intervention strategies must take this into account. Play activities may afford the young child an opportunity to express feelings and thoughts that are not expressed verbally. The use of clay, paint or building blocks may be a viable medium for preschool children.

Childhood (Ages 5 through 11)

- sadness & crying
- poor concentration
- fear of personal harm
- bed wetting
- confusion
- physical complaints (e.g., headaches)
- regressive behavior (clinging, whining)
- aggressive behavior at home or school
- withdrawal/social isolation
- attention-seeking behavior

- school avoidance
- irritability
- nightmares
- anxiety & fears
- eating difficulty

Interventions:

It is important to consider that children, especially younger children, typically do not have the ability to adequately express their feelings verbally. Consequently, the manifestation of these emotions are often behavioral and need a forum for ventilation. Most young children do not understand the finality of death and may deny its permanency. Children at the elementary level may develop genuine fears regarding death and fear separation from their families and friends.

Play sessions, in which feelings and thoughts can be expressed, should be considered. Planned discussion about fears and anxieties may also help. Painting or drawing, writing in a journal, reading and/or discussing stories, and exercising may all facilitate the healing process. Given the developmental level of verbal communication for most children in this age group, drawings, especially, seem to offer a safe and playful forum for the expression of emotion. The child could be asked to describe their drawing and/or tell a story. For instance, the child can be encouraged to draw what they are afraid of and the good things that they can remember about the incident (e.g., the police officer with the dog). It is important that the child is never blamed or judged for their reactions to the crisis.

Early Adolescence (Ages 11 through 14)

- sleep disturbance
- withdrawal/isolation from peers
- increase or decrease in appetite
- loss of interest in activities
- rebelliousness
- generalized anxiety
- school difficulty, including fighting
- fear of personal harm
- physical ailments (e.g., bowel problems)
- poor school performance
- depression
- concentration difficulties

Interventions:

Children at this age often exhibit concern regarding separation and non-existence. Speculation of what becomes of the deceased, once their body has expired, is possible. Young adolescents, especially boys, may display bravado and present as cynical, perhaps as a defense against overwhelming emotional reactions.

Group discussions that encourage the children to talk about their feelings regarding the crisis may be beneficial. Students at this age often express confusion about death and seek information. Issues about personal and family safety may be discussed. Teachers may encourage students to write a letter (e.g., to the families of victims, to rescue workers, etc.).

Additionally, they can say to their students:

- "It's OK to have the feelings that you have today."
- "Your reaction is a normal response to an abnormal event."
- "It's OK. not to be OK."
- "I am here for you if you would like to talk."

The creation of plays or stories with favorable outcomes could be beneficial. Such activities can promote a sense of mastery which helps mitigate feelings of helplessness and vulnerability which may abound at such times. Coping strategies such as relaxation techniques (e.g., deep breathing) and listening to music could be discussed and may help to further empower students. Assessment of the child's thoughts may indicate distorted perceptions and irrational beliefs (e.g., "Mom is going to die too."). Healthier and more adaptive thoughts can be developed with the youngster(s) and recorded on a piece of paper. The manner in which "happier" thoughts can create "happier" feelings can be described (for more information, see Forman, 1993; Meyers & Craighead, 1984). Temporary modification in school and homework assignments should be considered. More individualized attention may be needed for academic instruction.

Adolescence (Ages 14 through 18)

- intrusive recollections
- numbing
- anxiety and feelings of guilt
- sleep disturbance
- eating disturbance
- apathy
- antisocial behavior (e.g., stealing)
- aggressive behavior
- poor school performance
- depression
- increased substance abuse
- peer problems
- amenorrhea or dysmenorrhea
- withdrawal
- poor concentration and distractibility
- psychosomatic symptoms (e.g., headaches)
- agitation or decrease in energy level
- decreased interest in the opposite sex

Interventions:

Adolescents can usually engage in more abstract and hypothetical thinking and there is a better sense of the permanence of death. However, many teens maintain distorted cognitions that, this event could *never happen* to them and that "good things happen to good people and bad things happen to bad people." A crisis situation involving death challenges the thoughts that individuals have often developed by this age.

It is important to encourage discussion of feelings, beliefs and concerns regarding the crisis situation without insisting on this expression. Certain types of crises (e.g., death) tend to evoke memories of past loss and subsequently, negative emotions. Faulty thinking regarding the events may be addressed (e.g., "I should have saved him."). Look for common themes, beliefs and feelings among individuals. Strive to acknowledge and normalize these reactions. As indicated earlier, empathic listening to students in a non-judgmental and genuine fashion is essential. It is important to remain patient, especially when the individual is resistant to overt expression of their opinions and/or emotions.

Things that faculty could say include:

- "Given what you have been through, It's understandable that you feel this way."

- "It's not unusual to feel alone."

- "Things may seem very disorganized and chaotic right now, but things may become clearer with time."

- "Many people tend to blame themselves for things that they had absolutely no control over; do you think that is true here?"

- "I understand that these feelings can be uncomfortable and, at times, overwhelming."

- "Keep in mind that I'm here for you if you need me."

Maintain sensitivity to the adolescent's level of understanding. Moreover, do not assume that you should have all of the answers to his or her questions; say "I don't know" when it is deemed appropriate. Remember to respond honestly and directly.

Coping strategies such as relaxation techniques and problem-solving strategies may be discussed. Expectations for specific levels of school and home performance may need to be temporarily modified. A safe forum for ventilation may be provided by a class discussion or writing assignment. Some of the topic areas to consider may include:

- Losses that we have experienced in the past.

- Personal experiences with death and how we coped in the past.

- Feelings about loss or death.

- Things that we can do to take care of ourselves.

- What are the differences between grieving and depression?

Adulthood

• shock and disbelief	• denial
• feelings of detachment	• depression
• unwanted, intrusive recollections	• anxiety
• concentration difficulty	• hypervigilance
• psychosomatic complaints	• withdrawal
• eating disturbance	• sleep difficulty
• poor work performance	• emotional lability
• emotional and mental fatigue	• marital discord
• irritability and low frustration tolerance	
• loss of interest in activities once enjoyed	

Interventions:

Adults who are exposed to a crisis situation often experience feelings of vulnerability and helplessness. Faculty and staff who are exposed to a crisis are at risk of experiencing emotional distress related to the incident. For example, the teacher who has just learned that her colleague has died of a heart attack in the classroom next door may need immediate support. This individual's shock at this untimely news, his/her sense of aloneness and loss, and immediate well-being should be prioritized. The teacher should have the option, if possible, to leave his/her immediate classroom and seek the support of his/her colleagues and/or professional support staff. Referrals to outside professionals (e.g., psychologists) should be made by appropriate school personnel if warranted. As always, privacy and confidentiality are essential.

Allowing the person to share their experience (i.e., "tell their story") either on a one-to-one basis or in a small group setting is a useful strategy. Beliefs surrounding the event may be distorted and precipitate feelings of guilt, anxiety and depression. Other coping strategies may include:

- temporarily altering one's work schedule to decrease demands,
- seeking social support (e.g., colleagues, self-help groups),
- exercise such as jogging, walking, bicycling,
- relaxation exercises such as yoga, meditation,
- maintaining a balanced diet and sleep cycle,
- writing about the experience,
- listening to music, and
- hot baths and massage.

Chapter 11 will will explore specific strategies for helping caregivers to take care of themselves.

Summary of Intervention Strategies

Preschool and Elementary Children

- Play activities including the use of clay or blocks
- Painting
- Drawing pictures reflecting feelings and memories
- Writing in a journal (for older children)
- Reading and discussing stories
- Writing cards or letters to the deceased or surviving family members (if applicable)
- Creating a mural or "memory board" about their experiences during the crisis
- Developing a "memory box" to process "happy" thoughts
- Develop "thoughts as they relate to feelings" chart
- Individual and group counseling

Adolescents

- Journal writing
- Art activities
- Poetry writing
- Story writing
- Writing cards or letters to the deceased or surviving family members (if applicable)
- Relaxation techniques including deep breathing and muscle relaxation
- Problem-solving strategies
- Small group discussions
- Support groups
- Exercise
- Listening to music
- Individual and group counseling

Adults

- Temporarily alter work schedule
- Seek social support
- Exercise
- Relaxation exercises such as yoga and meditation
- Writing about the experience
- Listening to music
- Hot baths and massage
- Individual and group counseling

CHAPTER SIX

Practical Information Concerning Grief Counseling

Grief refers to the feelings that are precipitated by loss. Loss may take different forms including the loss of a personally meaningful relationship or the loss of an attachment figure. Moreover, secondary losses include aspects of life that are lost as a consequence of another loss (Baker & Sedney, 1996). These losses involve the way in which life changes after a death such as the need to move to a new home, changes in routine (e.g., child care) and perhaps, changing schools.

Bowlby (1980) identified four factors that will affect a child's ability to grieve or mourn a loss and should be considered by school personnel who attempt to offer support to children and adolescents. A child can begin the process of mourning if they:

- maintained a secure relationship to their parents/caregivers before the death/loss,

- receive prompt and precise information about the death/loss,

- are participants (if they desire) in the social rituals following the loss/death (e.g., funeral) and

- have access to significant others in the days and months following the loss/death.

It is essential that school personnel and caregivers understand that coping with loss is a process involving a series of tasks carried out over time (Baker, Sedney, & Gross, 1992). The passage of time is a necessary but not a sufficient component of successful grieving.

Helping Preschool and Elementary Children Cope with Loss

Children must feel safe before they can begin to grieve. Grieving involves "emotional risk-taking" for the individual. Baker and Sedney (1996) have emphasized the importance of providing children with accurate information that they can comprehend. Children can benefit from knowing about the "story" of how the person or persons died, why the person or persons died, and when the death occurred. Of course, the explanation provided will depend upon the age of the child.

It is important to consider that deaths that occur through traumatic or violent circumstances may prolong the time that the child takes to feel safe in their world. Moreover, traumatic reactions including sleep and eating disturbances, concentration impairment and withdrawal must be addressed before grieving can successfully occur. Thus, referral to and support from the child's pediatrician or mental health providers in the community should be considered depending on the circumstances.

Acceptance of a loss at cognitive and emotional levels is a process that will vary considerably from individual to individual. Factors affecting acceptance of loss include the bereaved child's history of prior losses, family and social support, and the manner in which significant others react to the child. Children may ask questions repetitively in their effort to find answers for their loss. This reflects their feelings of confusion and uncertainty. It is essential to understand that a child does not fully understand the finality and irreversibility of death until 6 or 7 years of age. Consequently, asking questions regarding when the bereaved will be "returning" or seemingly "forgetting" that they were told that the dead person(s) will not be returning are common responses.

At approximately 10 years of age, children begin to understand that death is universal, irreversible and inevitable (Baker & Sedney, 1996). Feelings of guilt and anger may be coupled with anxiety and depression as the child processes the loss and comes to greater acceptance of the change in their life situation.

Helping Adolescents Cope with Loss

Noppe and Noppe (1996) have suggested that adolescents may be especially vulnerable to conflict and tension that follow the death of a significant other. Adolescents understand that death eventually occurs for all living things (i.e., universality) and that death is irreversible. When a tragic death does occur, teens may exhibit a cascade of emotions ranging from rage to complete withdrawal.

It is important to understand that when teens lose a friend, for example, there is a loss of companionship, loss of an important confidant, love and personal support (Oltjenbruns, 1996). Thus, considerable challenges to one's sense of security and safety may ensue. The death of a friend or significant other may also affect the adolescent's sense of self-identity. Thus, integrating the concept of mortality into one's conceptions about their world may be a necessary but formidable task.

> When a tragic death does occur, teens may exhibit a cascade of emotions ranging from rage to complete withdrawal.

"Survivor guilt" may also complicate the process of bereavement and acceptance of loss for the adolescent such that a belief is maintained that one should have died with or instead of the person who died (Oltjenbruns, 1996). This may be especially relevant when one is responsible for the death of their friend or significant other (e.g., motor vehicle accident). Again, if bereavement is complicated by traumatic reactions to a loss, referral to and support from mental health providers in the community should be considered depending on the circumstances.

Phases of the Grieving Process

It is essential to consider that there is variation from person to person concerning how quickly an individual will move through the tasks associated with grieving or mourning. The following is a brief outline describing some of the reactions by people who experience a significant loss (Bowlby, 1980; Kubler-Ross, 1969). Hill and Foster (1996) indicate that people do not necessarily progress sequentially and linearly through these phases and new losses may begin the process from the beginning all over again.

I. Numbing (Initial reaction)
- Shock and denial (e.g., "I can't believe it... It's a bad dream... It's not happening to me...")
- Periods of intense emotion (e.g., anger, rage, guilt, fear)

II. Yearning & Searching (Within hours or days)
- Beginning to register reality of the loss
- Preoccupation with lost individual
- Symptoms of insomnia, poor appetite, headaches, anxiety, tension, anger...
- Sounds and signals interpreted as deceased person's presence

III. Disorganization (Weeks to months following)
- Feelings of anger and depression
- Questioning (e.g., "Why did this have to happen?")
- Bargaining (e.g., "If only I could see him just one last time....")

IV. Reorganization (Months to years following)
- Acceptance
- New patterns and goals

Assisting Students During Specific Grieving Situations

Life-Threatening Illness of a Classmate

Children and adolescents are, at times, subjected to the death of a classmate in their school system as a result of life-threatening diseases (e.g., terminal illness). Unlike other deaths, such a condition may be known to students and staff. There are several strategies to consider in preparation for a loss and after the loss of a peer.

Prior to Death

- Give careful consideration to the wishes of the child.

- Receive and clarify information about the child's health status with the permission of the child and his/her parent or guardian.

- Educate students about the disease in terms they can understand (depending upon the age of student).

- As long as possible, keep the ill student involved in classroom activities and projects.

- Assist the ill student in expressing his or her own needs.

- Be familiar with the Crisis Response Plan of the school building/district.

After Death

- Upon death of the student, have support personnel in the classroom to offer assistance.

- If possible, facilitate discussion about thoughts and feelings associated with the loss.

- Have students write a card for the student's family.

- Consider funeral attendance (use discretion and consider the age of the child).

- Consider the needs and wishes of the family regarding phone calls to the home.

- Identify students who were particularly close to the child and make referrals for outside assistance if indicated.

Death of a Parent/Guardian

A child who loses a caregiver will undoubtedly experience a significant impact on his or her functioning in the school and home settings. Some suggestions for assisting students who lose a parent/guardian include:

- Reassure the student of his/her safety and security at school.

- Modify academic expectations and assignments temporarily.

- Provide opportunities for ventilation of emotions.

- Educate the student of reactions that they may experience over the next few weeks and/or months (e.g., sleep difficulty, anger, etc.).

- Provide the student with an opportunity to reminisce and reflect on their deceased significant other.
- Offer in-school counseling (i.e., bereavement group).
- Assist with out-of-school interventions/referrals if indicated.

Concluding Comments and Summary

Loss and grief will have a tremendous impact on children and adolescents emotionally, academically and behaviorally. School performance may be hampered by shorter attention span, irritability, acting out, increased need for teacher attention, and feelings of anger, guilt, anxiety and profound sadness. In general, increased support including individual and family counseling, bereavement support groups, journalizing, poetry and art therapy should be explored as methods for assisting individuals with the bereavement process.

There are no "cookbook" approaches to counseling individuals who are struggling with loss. Perhaps, the most important factor is "being there" for the person. Attempt to develop a "helping relationship" that is characterized by empathy, warmth and genuineness. Encouragement to express feeling without insistence is recommended. **Although relatives and friends intend to be supportive, they may be inclined to discourage the expression of feelings, particularly anger and guilt. Avoidance of such expression for individuals may prolong the grieving process and can be counterproductive.** Allow for periods of silence and be careful not to lecture. It is also important to avoid cliches such as "Be strong..." and "You are doing so well...." Such cliches may only serve to reinforce an individual's feelings of aloneness. Again, allow the bereaved to tell you how *they* feel and attempt to "normalize" grief reactions by discussing (as needed) reactions that they may encounter as they attempt to recover from the loss (see aforementioned phases of mourning). Finally, do not be afraid to offer a comforting touch. A squeeze of the hand or a gentle pat on the back can demonstrate for the individual that you are there and that you truly care.

CHAPTER SEVEN

Managing "Everyday Crises" in the School Setting

I. Domestic Violence

In the past two decades, there has been growing recognition of the prevalence of domestic violence in our society. Moreover, it has become apparent that some individuals are at greater risk for victimization than others. Domestic violence has adverse effects on children, families, and society in general.

Domestic violence includes physical abuse, sexual abuse, psychological abuse, and abuse to property and pets (Ganley, 1989). Exposure to this form of violence has considerable potential to be perceived as life-threatening by those victimized and can leave them with a sense of vulnerability, helplessness, and in extreme cases, horror. **Physical abuse** refers to any behavior that involves the intentional use of force against the body of another person that risks physical injury, harm, and/or pain (Dutton, 1992). Physical abuse includes pushing, hitting, slapping, choking, using an object to hit, twisting of a body part, forcing the ingestion of an unwanted substance, and use of a weapon. **Sexual abuse** is defined as any unwanted sexual intimacy forced on one individual by another. It may include oral, anal, penile or vaginal stimulation or penetration, forced nudity, forced exposure to sexually explicit material or activity, or any other unwanted sexual activity (Dutton, 1994). Compliance may be obtained through actual or threatened physical force or through some other form of coercion. **Psychological abuse** may include derogatory statements or threats of further abuse (e.g., threats of being killed by another individual). It may also involve isolation, economic threats and emotional abuse.

Prevalence of Domestic Violence

Domestic violence is widespread and occurs among all socioeconomic groups. Survey data from the United States and Canada suggest that domestic violence occurs in approximately 28% of all marriages (Center for the Prevention of Sexual and Domestic Violence, 2002). In a national study of over 6,000 American families, it was estimated that between 53% and 70% of male batterers (i.e., they assaulted their wives) also frequently abused their children (Straus & Gelles, 1990). Other research suggests that women who have been hit by their husbands were twice as likely as other women to abuse a child (CWP, 1995).

Survey data from the United States and Canada suggest that domestic violence occurs in approximately 28% of all marriages

The risks of exposure to parental violence is increasing. Children from homes where domestic violence occurs are physically or sexually abused and/or seriously neglected at a rate 15 times the national average (McKay, 1994). Approximately, 45% to 70% of battered women in shelters have reported the presence of child abuse in their home (Meichenbaum, 1994). About two-thirds of abused children are being parented by battered women (McKay, 1994). Of the abused children, they are three times more likely to have been abused by their fathers.

Studies of the incidence of physical and sexual violence in the lives of children suggest that this form of violence can be viewed as a serious public health problem. In 2000, approximately 879,000 children were found to be victims of child maltreatment including neglect, medical neglect, physical abuse, sexual abuse, and psychological maltreatment. In fact, two-thirds of child victims (63%) suffered neglect (including medical neglect), 19 percent were physically abused, 10 percent were sexually abused, and 8 percent were psychologically maltreated (National Child Abuse and Neglect Data System, 2002). It has been estimated that about 1 in 5 female children and 1 in 10 male children may experience sexual molestation (Regier & Cowdry, 1995).

Signs and Symptoms of Domestic Violence in Children and Adolescents

More than half of the school-age children in domestic violence shelters show clinical levels of anxiety or Posttraumatic Stress Disorder (Graham-Bermann, 1994). Without treatment, these children are at significant risk for delinquency, substance abuse, school drop-out, and difficulties in their own relationships.

Children may exhibit a wide range of reactions to exposure to violence in their home. Younger children (e.g., preschool and kindergarten) oftentimes do not understand the meaning of the abuse they observe and tend to believe that they "must have done something wrong." Self-blame can precipitate feelings of guilt, worry, and anxiety. **It is important to consider that children, especially younger children, typically do not have the ability to adequately express their feelings verbally. Consequently, the manifestation of these emotions are often behavioral.** Children may become withdrawn, non-verbal, and exhibit regressed behaviors such as clinging and whining. Eating and sleeping difficulty, concentration problems, generalized anxiety, and physical complaints (e.g., headaches) are all common.

> **Children, especially younger children, typically do not have the ability to adequately express their feelings verbally. Consequently, the manifestation of these emotions are often behavioral.**

Unlike younger children, the pre-adolescent child typically has greater ability to verbalize negative emotions. In addition to symptoms commonly seen with childhood anxiety (e.g., sleep problems, eating disturbance, nightmares), victims within this age group may show a loss of interest in social activities, low self-concept, withdrawal or avoidance of peer relations, rebelliousness and oppositional-defiant behavior in the school setting. It is also common to observe temper tantrums, irritability, frequent fighting at school or between siblings, lashing out at objects, treating pets cruelly or abusively, threatening of peers or siblings with violence (e.g., "Give me a pen or I will smack you!"), and attempts to gain attention through hitting, kicking, or choking peers and/or family members. Incidentally, girls are more likely to exhibit withdrawal and unfortunately, run the risk of being "missed" as a child in need of support.

Adolescents are at risk of academic failure, school drop-out, delinquency, and substance abuse. Some investigators have suggested that a history of family violence or abuse is the most significant difference between delinquent and nondelinquent youth.

An estimated 1/5 to 1/3 of all teenagers who are involved in dating relationships are regularly abusing or being abused by their partners verbally, mentally, emotionally, sexually, and/or physically (SASS, 1996). Between 30% and 50% of dating relationships can exhibit the same cycle of escalating violence as marital relationships (SASS, 1996).

Assisting Children and Adolescents Exposed to Domestic Violence

For some children and adolescents, questions about home life may be difficult to answer, especially if the individual has been "warned" or threatened by a family member to refrain from "talking to strangers" about events that have taken place in the family. Therefore, the student may require an extended period of time to disclose important information. Referrals to the appropriate school personnel could be the first step in assisting the child or teen in need of support. When there is suggestion of domestic violence with a student, consider involving the school psychologist, social worker, guidance counselor and/or a school administrator (when indicated). Although the circumstances surrounding each case may vary, suspicion of child abuse is required to be reported to the local child protection agency by teachers and other school personnel. In some cases, a contact with the local police department may also be necessary. When in doubt, consult with school team members.

If the child expresses a desire to talk, provide them with an opportunity to express their thoughts and feelings. In addition to talking, they may be also encouraged to write in a journal, draw, or paint; these are all viable means for facilitating expression in younger children. Adolescents are typically more abstract in their thinking and generally have better developed verbal abilities than younger children. It could be helpful for adults who work with teenagers to encourage them to talk about their concerns without insisting on this expression. Listening in a warm, non-judgmental, and genuine manner is often comforting for victims and may be an important first step in their seeking further support. When appropriate, individual and/or group counseling should be considered at school if the individual is amenable. Referrals for counseling (e.g., family counseling) outside of the school should be made to the family as well. Providing a list of names and phone numbers to contact in case of a serious crisis can be helpful.

II. The Suicidal Student

Suicide is the third leading cause of death among people 15 to 24 years of age, following accidents and homicide with the number of adolescents who commit suicide significantly increasing over the past few decades (National Center for Health Statistics, 2000). According to the American Foundation for Suicide Prevention (1998), suicide rates vary with the age group examined. Suicide in younger children is actually quite uncommon with children under the age of 10 accounting for the smallest amount of suicides. Suicide for children between the ages of 10 and 14 accounts for approximately 7% of all deaths occurring in this age group in the United States and less that 2% of all suicides across all age groups. It is important to note that the suicide rate for children, 10 to 14 years old has, however, more than doubled over the last 15 years.

> **Adolescent females are more likely to attempt suicide whereas males are more likely to successfully commit suicide**

Adolescents attempt suicide at a much higher rate than they actually complete the act. **Adolescent females are more likely to attempt suicide whereas males are more likely to successfully commit suicide (i.e., they tend to use more lethal means).** Guns, especially handguns, are the most frequent cause of successfully completed suicides. Suicide attempts are typically manifested as drug overdoses and occur in the home (Kovacs, Goldston & Gatsonis, 1993).

Children and adolescents not only make suicide attempts (often referred to as parasuicidal behavior) but also think about suicide. Between 16% and 30% of children referred for clinical services who manifest suicidal thoughts actually attempt it (Kovacs et al., 1993).

Presentation of the Suicidal Student

A review of the scientific literature indicates that a number of family and individual variables should be evaluated when determining suicidal risk (Fremouw, de Perczel & Ellis, 1990; Range, 1996). These variables follow:

Family Variables Related to Higher Risk

- Higher levels of family discord/conflict (i.e., lack of cohesion)
- Family history of depression and/or mental illness
- Lack of emotional support
- Illicit drug and alcohol use among family members
- Sexual and/or physical abuse or neglect suspected within the family
- Family stress including parental unemployment, divorce and family relocation
- Family history of suicide

Individual Variables Related to Higher Risk

- Mood disorders, especially depression
- Feelings of hopelessness
- Sleep and/or eating difficulties
- Anger, aggressive tendencies and hostility
- Conduct problems including running away
- Substance use and abuse (e.g., alcohol and illicit drugs)
- Poor problem-solving skills
- More negative life events (e.g., recent loss)
- School problems (e.g., academic failure, behavior problems)
- Prior psychiatric hospitalization
- History of self-destructive behavior/suicide attempt(s)
- Difficulty promising that they would not harm self
- Unusual neglect of personal appearance
- Impulsivity
- Anxiety/Panic-related symptoms
- Eating disorders
- Sudden tendencies toward isolative and withdrawn behavior

The student who presents with a desire to end his/her life will need immediate attention. Individuals who are actively suicidal often exhibit multiple signs of distress. These signs may include:

- saying farewell to peers
- giving away prized possessions,
- writing essays and/or notes about suicide
- verbalizing to a peer or teacher about "not wanting to be around any longer"
- excessive fatigue
- sudden changes in personality and
- self-destructive behavior (e.g., self-mutilation).

Related Information for the Management of a Suicidal Crisis

Self-mutilation, cutting and/or skin carving are not always indicative of suicidal intention. Such behaviors may be observed with concomitant psychopathology including depression, complex forms of Posttraumatic Stress Disorder and personality disorders. Thus, intervention for self-mutilating behavior should be addressed accordingly and should involve consultation with the school nurse.

In-school counseling, psychotherapy and/or psychiatric consultation are typically recommended to the student and their family to address related issues.

If a student attempts suicide on school grounds, immediate contact with school administrators and the police is recommended. Building security should be involved and work collaboratively with local law enforcement to safeguard students and staff in the area. Security guards can engage in crowd control and allow emergency support personnel to intervene. Individuals who witness a suicide attempt will need careful monitoring and support to help mitigate the effects of exposure to such a traumatic event.

The Management of Suicidal Students

Threats of suicide must be taken seriously. Such verbalization and actions are not "simple" means for individuals to "get attention." These students are oftentimes desperately seeking help and will need support. The actively suicidal student's judgement is often impaired and they may have no insight into the notion that "suicide is a permanent solution to a temporary problem" (Fremouw, de Perczel & Ellis, 1990).

It is important to always have face-to-face contact with the suicidal teenager. Do not attempt to exclusively evaluate through indirect methods (e.g., through peer observation or staff report only). Direct interview of the student in a safe and non-threatening environment is recommended.

Discussing the possibility of suicide with the student does not increase the likelihood that he or she will commit suicide. The school staff member (e.g., school psychologist or social worker) who is working with the student should never attempt to manage a suicidal student alone. They should work in a collaborative fashion with a colleague, perhaps, the school administrator, school nurse, guidance counselor, teacher or adult who may be more familiar with the student to facilitate the evaluative process.

Questions and interaction with the student should be made in a calm and quiet manner and without overt expressions of shock or disbelief conveyed to the student. Do not portray questions euphemistically (e.g., "Why do you want to meet your maker?" or "Why do you want to go to Heaven?"). Start questions relatively general and then get more specific. Be direct (e.g., "Why do you want to kill yourself?"). Practical interview questions include:

- Have you been feeling depressed? Adjust language depending on age (e.g., sad, bummed-out, blue...).
- How long have you been feeling depressed?
- Do you feel that everything is hopeless?
- Have you experienced difficulty sleeping?
  (e.g., falling asleep versus middle of night awakening?)

- Has your appetite changed (e.g., Have you gained or lost weight?)
- Have you found yourself turning to alcohol or other substances to help you cope?
- During this time, have you ever had thoughts of killing yourself?
- When did these thoughts occur?
- What did you think about doing to yourself?
- Did you act on your thoughts?
- What stopped you from doing it?
- How often have these thoughts occurred?
- When was the last time you had these thoughts?
- Can you promise that you will not harm yourself?
- Have your thoughts ever included harming someone else in addition to yourself?
- How often has that occurred?
- What have you thought about doing to the other person or people?
- Have you taken any steps toward acquiring the gun, pills, etc.?
- Have you thought about when/where you would do this?
- Have you thought about the effect that your death would have on your family or friends?
- What help could make it easier for you to cope with your current thoughts and plans?
- What makes you want to live?
- How does talking about this make you feel?

It is essential to determine the frequency and duration of suicidal ideation and suicidal intention. If suicidal thinking is reported, then an assessment of suicidal intent must be conducted. A suicidal plan should be investigated. This will include ascertaining information regarding:

- the *means* or method that one would utilize to kill himself or herself
- the *availability* or access that the individual has to the stated means
- the *lethality* or likelihood of success given the chosen suicidal method
- the *intent* or how probable the individual is to follow through on the act

More severe risk is indicated when there is a greater magnitude of family and individual variables present and when specific plans including available and lethal means are reported (Fremouw, de Perczel & Ellis, 1990). Self-report instruments such as the Children's Depression Inventory (CDI; Kovaks & Beck, 1977), Reynolds Adolescent Depression Scale -2nd Ed. (RADS-2; Reynolds, 2002) or Suicide Ideation Questionnaire (Reynolds, 1987) may be used to supplement information obtained through the interview method but should never be used as the sole criterion for determining suicidal risk.

Contact with parents or legal guardians should always be made. In such circumstances, pledges of confidentiality can not be kept (e.g., a promise not to inform a parent of the student's suicidal ideation or intent). Harboring such information can be potentially dangerous. In certain circumstances, a "No Suicide" contract may be indicated. This would be developed in an effort to delay self-destructive actions by the student. However, it should not be done as a substitute for contacting significant others. This is especially the case with the greater number of risk factors indicated. Discuss with the parent/guardian:

- the seriousness of the situation

- the specific intention or plan of the individual

- the need for close monitoring

- the need to remove weapons (e.g., firearms), illicit substances including alcohol and/or potentially dangerous prescription drugs from the house

- the need for psychiatric evaluation and/or hospitalization

If the student is presenting as a danger to himself or herself, hospital admission should be considered. Using discretion, the need for support of the local police department or mobile crisis unit (if available) should be evaluated. Outside counseling (i.e., individual and/or family therapy) and psychiatric consultation are typically indicated and referrals for assistance should be recommended to the family. Follow-up including in-school counseling should be available to the student, especially upon return to school following the crisis. School support staff should obtain consent from parents/guardians to work in concert with outside support professionals as the student transitions back to their regular routine. As always privacy and/or confidentiality should be a high priority. A card with "suicide hot-lines" should be provided to possibly avert future crises. **School staff should be alerted of possible "contagion effects" following a suicide or suicide attempt by a student. In such situations, a peer or peers may present with suicidal ideation/ intent after exposure to a suicidal crisis (e.g., peer suicide or mass media/news stories).** Intervention should be implemented as necessary.

III. The Violent Student

Although some of the statistical data involving the trend toward a decrease in violence in our society is encouraging, violent behavior continues to have a presence in the school setting.

It has been suggested that individuals between the ages of 12 and 24 have the highest risk of becoming a victim of violence (APA, 1999). Moreover, the prevalence of certain types of crimes in the school environment has not changed. Between 1993 and 1999, the percentage of students in the United States in grades 9 through 12 who were threatened or injured with a weapon on school property remained constant (U.S. Department of Justice, 2001). Violent behavior is often the result of numerous contributing factors including faulty learning, poor coping skills and problem-solving abilities, anger/hostility, attempts to control other individuals, peer pressure, exposure to abuse/neglect in the home, psychopathology including depression and impulse-control difficulties.

It is important to consider that aggression in children, if unaddressed, can become a relatively stable trait over time (Olweus, 1984). Violent and aggressive behavior produces significant social adjustment difficulties for the perpetrator and is disruptive to the school community in general.

Presentation of the Violent Student

School personnel will oftentimes learn that a student is potentially violent through:

- direct observations of aggressive or violent behavior (e.g., the teacher who observes such behavior in the classroom),

- speaking with potentially violent students (i.e., the student may report their hatred and desire to be violent toward a peer, etc.),

- indirect means (e.g., writing assignments with violent or assaultive and/or homicidal themes, threatening e-mail), or

- peer reports.

It will be especially important to be aware of factors that place some individuals at higher risk for violent behavior. These factors may include:

- frequent loss of temper,

- numerous disciplinary actions at school (e.g., fighting),

- histories of aggression toward people and animals,

- tendencies toward bullying, threatening or intimidating others,

- substance use and abuse,

- isolative and withdrawn behavior,
- detailed plans to commit an act of violence,
- verbal or written expressions of hatred or anger or threats to hurt other individuals,
- deliberate acts of vandalism and destruction of property,
- gang involvement,
- feelings of rejection and/or alienation from peers,
- truancy,
- academic difficulties, and
- access to weapons including firearms and knives.

Strategies for Managing the Violent Student

Students who are violent pose a significant threat to their own well-being as well as that of the school community. These students should be seen as soon as school personnel become aware of the issue. With regard to the aforementioned risk factors, as the number of factors increases, so does the need for intervention become more imminent (See Practical Document E).

The needs of the violent student must be addressed. As always, consultation with school administration as well as parents and/or guardians is essential. If the student has a specific plan to engage in an act of violence toward another person, contact with the police or local law enforcement agency should be strongly considered. Using discretion, contact with the intended target may be necessary.

When a student (or students) presents as agitated, encourage the individual to sit down. This will reduce the probability of the student(s) striking out physically. Whenever possible, position yourself between the student and an exit. Then, provide the student(s) with the opportunity to "tell his/her story." Attempt to convey empathy (i.e., that you are trying to understand and appreciate their circumstance). In cases where students are agitated due to interpersonal conflicts, make every effort to separate the disputing parties.

Physical force or restraining of students should only be utilized when the safety of the student or others is compromised and there are no other options. As always, make every effort to work collaboratively with school personnel when working with the agitated and potentially violent student. After the immediate crisis is resolved and a potentially violent situation is defused, then a referral to school administration should be entertained for possible disciplinary action.

In-school counseling and outside professional counseling are typically recommended as a means for intervention. The individual may have an opportunity to explore:

- anger control techniques,

- social skills training,

- assertion skills,

- self-management skills including training in self-talk or self-instruction,

- communication skills, and

- relaxation techniques.

Family counseling is often suggested as a means to assist communication styles and/or conflict that may exist in the homes of "at risk" students. If substance abuse is a related factor, then treatment should also focus on abstinence and relapse prevention training. In-school counseling as well as group counseling should be considered as means of developing alternate coping strategies. Recognize that not all violent students and their families will be receptive to the school's efforts to intervene. Under such circumstances, administrative action (e.g., expulsion, home-bound instruction) may need to be implemented.

Students who are the victims of violence may need special attention as well. Beginning in the elementary level, students should be educated about factors (i.e., warning signs) related to violent behavior. Students need to learn the signs or "red flags" for violent behavior to help themselves if they encounter these problems or know of someone who does. They should be informed that they have the right to feel safe in their school environment and that intimidating or bullying behavior is not tolerated at school. Students should be informed that there are school staff members that they can privately approach in the event that they are victims of violence or suspect that a peer is potentially violent. Students should be advised to avoid conflict by minimizing their exposure to violent peers. They should be reminded that being alone with such individuals is a possible risk for them especially if the person exhibits various warning signs for violent behavior.

IV. The Substance Abusing Student

According to the National Household Survey on Drug Abuse (NHSDA, 2001), approximately 16.6 million Americans aged 12 or older were diagnosed with dependence on or abuse of either alcohol or illicit drugs (i.e., 7.3% of the total population). Between 2000 and 2001, there was a significant increase in the number of individuals 12 or older in need of treatment for an illicit drug problem (NHSDA, 2001).

In a large scale survey conducted by the Substance Abuse and Mental Health Services Administration (1994), it was reported that marijuana, tobacco, and alcohol account for a large proportion of reported drug use. Marijuana is the most commonly used illicit substance with heavy alcohol use reported by 5.7% of the population aged 12 or older (NHSDA, 2001).

Almost two-thirds of all American youth try illicit drugs before completion of high school and almost 90% have tried alcohol, a popular "gateway" drug for many adolescents (Anderson, 1998). Other abused substances include cocaine, crack, crank, heroin, MDMA or "Ecstasy," phencyclidine, methaqualone, Oxycontin, and hallucinogens. Abuse is also observed with legal drugs not prescribed by a physician including amphetamines, benzodiazepines, barbiturates and anabolic steroids and inhalants such as amyl and butyl nitrite, gasoline, nitrous oxide, glue and other solvents.

> **Almost two-thirds of all American youth try illicit drugs before completion of high school**

Presentation of the Substance Abusing Student

The drugs that young people are using today are stronger, purer, cheaper to produce and purchase (Gonet, 1994). Moreover, they are readily available. The student who presents as substance abusing will oftentimes, show evidence in the school setting of deterioration in academic and social functioning. Warning signs include:

- School failure
- Frequent lateness
- Frequent absences
- Forgetfulness
- Concentration difficulties
- Blackouts (or drug-induced amnesia)
- Excessively and easily angered and hostile
- Erratic mood swings
- Depression
- Changes in friends and relationships
- Defiance of rules
- Unkempt physical appearance
- Excessive weight gain or loss
- Frequent lying
- Legal problems
- Excessive disciplinary referrals at school
- Loss of initiative
- Isolation and secretiveness

- Argumentativeness and defensiveness

- Paranoia

- Family discord

- Parental substance abuse

- Disappearance of money or valuables from home or from others

- Watery or red eyes with dilated pupils

- Excessive use of eye-drops (e.g., Visine® or other over-the-counter products)

- Deodorizers for room

- Drug paraphernalia including matches, pipes, screens, rolling paper, scales, seeds and small bags

Strategies for Managing the Substance Abusing Student

In order to assess the needs of a student suspected of abusing drugs, at the very least, a careful diagnostic interview should be conducted. The school psychologist or social worker is in the best position to perform this evaluation given their training and expertise. Information about the type(s) of substance(s) that are being used, frequency of use, amounts being consumed and effects that the substance(s) has had on functioning should be addressed. The student may present as guarded and defensive in light of your questioning. Remain calm and make every effort to protect the individual's confidentiality and privacy.

Although substance use during the school day is a violation of school rules/policy, disciplinary action should be deferred until the substance abuse is addressed with the family of these youngsters.

If an individual is impaired and not fit for educational instruction, schools should evaluate their district policy regarding the handling of such matters. Teachers should consult with the school psychologist, social worker, nurse and/or administrators so as to be informed on how to proceed with the youngster. **An evaluation by the school nurse for vital signs including heart rate, blood pressure, temperature and pupil response should be routine.** Contact with parent or guardians is usually indicated in these circumstances. The student may need further assessment by their family physician or pediatrician. Although substance use during the school day is a violation of school rules/policy, disciplinary action should be deferred until the substance abuse is addressed with the family of these youngsters.

Some students may exhibit behaviors (e.g., poor school performance, mood lability) consistent with drug use or abuse. However, the student may deny any usage. In these situations, parent involvement is essential in order to address the problem. A parent conference is recommended to discuss intervention strategies.

Recommendations for intervention may include:

- Medical assessment
- Toxicologic tests [using radioimmunoassays (RIA) or enzymatic immunoassay (EIA)]
- Individual and group counseling within school setting
- Substance abuse counseling (outside of school)
- Family counseling
- Drug education courses
- Day treatment programs
- Residential programs

By intervening early with substance abusing students, the long-term costs to the individual, his or her family and society can be kept to a minimum. Many students will relapse and go through treatment several times before they have a full recovery. Individuals who follow treatment plans as prescribed by professionals have better prognoses for a more efficient recovery. For those students who return from outside substance abuse programs, a supportive recovery environment involving family and non-substance abusing peers, is strongly indicated. The school district should work collaboratively with such programs to facilitate transitioning back to the regular school routine. In-school counseling and support should be available as needed to help with relapse prevention.

V. The Pregnant Adolescent

According to national statistics, a decrease in the percentage of all high school aged adolescents (9th through 12th grade) who have had sexual intercourse and an increase in the rate of contraceptive use have likely contributed to lowered teen pregnancy rates in recent years (The Henry J. Kaiser Family Foundation, 2000). However, approximately 900,000 pregnancies will occur each year among American teenagers aged 15 through 19 years old with most of these pregnancies unintended. Currently about 190,000 adolescents aged 17 and younger have children and their babies are often of lower birth weight. Younger mothers have disproportionately high infant mortality rates and are also far more likely to be poor (USDHHS, 2002). Additionally, as many as four million teens will contract a sexually transmitted disease (STD) every year (The Henry J. Kaiser Family Foundation, 2000).

Abstaining from sexual intercourse is truly the most effective method of preventing pregnancy and sexually transmitted diseases (STDs) according to Planned Parenthood (1998). However, given that experimentation, impulsivity and curiosity often guide adolescent decision-making, abstinence is often not the chosen course of prevention by many teens. Sexuality education is a viable but controversial topic in the United States. In the United States, almost half of teens report that they personally need more information on how to prevent AIDS and STDs (Princeton Survey Research Associates, 1996). Currently, there is no federal law or policy that mandates sex education or HIV education in the school (Sexuality Information and Education Council of the U.S., 2001).

Strategies for Assisting the Pregnant Adolescent

It is important to consider that younger mothers are at greater risk of health complications. This is typically due to inadequate prenatal care, poor nutrition, and unhealthy life-styles (Planned Parenthood, 1998). Pregnant teens are at high risk for academic failure, social difficulties and financial problems. When a school staff member becomes aware of a pregnancy with a student, contact with the student is essential. Consultation and perhaps, collaboration with the school nurse is strongly suggested given the expertise of the nurse with physical and/or medical-related issues. Interview of the student should include:

- obtaining information about the student's last menstrual cycle

- assessment of nutritional intake

- an evaluation of the student's health and psychological well-being

- physical examination

- plans of the individual regarding her pregnancy (e.g., keeping baby, etc.)

Laws in the United States governing parental contact for students under age 18 may vary and depend upon the state. As with any student who presents with risk of their health and/or well-being, contact with parents or guardians may be critical. It is best to first encourage the student to inform their parent. If student compliance is difficult, school contact may be indicated, especially with students under age 16.

Most teens who become pregnant will involve a parent in their decision to keep, adopt or abort their unborn child (Planned Parenthood, 1998). Twenty-five states currently have laws that mandate parental consent, parental notice or professional counseling for a minor to receive an abortion (Planned Parenthood, 1998). Students who elect to have an abortion will likely need additional support.

Empathic listening with the pregnant adolescent is critical. Emotionally, they are likely to be quite fragile and perhaps, irritable and moody. It is important to remember that this is an unexpected ordeal for most teenagers. The student and their family will need consistent support and counseling as they choose the best course of action. In some cases, alternate programs for pregnant teens can be considered.

VI. The Student Experiencing a Divorce

Divorce often comes unexpectedly for children and is often associated with intense emotions for those involved with the divorce process. Between a third and half of all children born in marriages will encounter a divorce and reside with a single parent prior to turning 18 years old (Acklin, 1998). The average divorce occurs within the first 7 years of marriage and consequently, many of these children are under the age of 6 (American Academy of Pediatrics, 1994). Children can thrive in a divorced home when provided with proper support and attention.

> **Between a third and half of all children born in marriages will encounter a divorce and reside with a single parent prior to turning 18 years old.**

Presentation of the Student Experiencing a Divorce

When parents present to their children that they are divorcing, children, depending on their age, will need time to process this potentially overwhelming information. Divorce is traumatic for many children. Although the details will typically be unclear, especially for younger children, the process of accepting this dramatic change will be manifested in a variety of ways.

According to the American Academy of Pediatrics (1994), a critical factor governing the effects of divorce on a child is how the parents are treating one another and the children during and after the divorce. Some parents will not put their children first in these matters and force a child to take sides in the divorce. Some parents will criticize each other in front of the children or have hostile conversations with the children present. Other parents will involve their child in their arguments between them. All of these circumstances will add a tremendous amount of unnecessary stress to an already traumatic situation.

Preschool children may experience the following reactions:

- Self-blame and a sense of responsibility
- Nightmares
- Anger and/or hostility
- Defiance
- Regressive behaviors including bed-wetting
- Fearfulness and/or separation anxiety
- Eating and/or sleeping difficulty
- Outbursts or tantrums

Elementary age children may experience the following reactions:

- Sleeping and/or eating difficulty
- Moodiness and irritability
- Feelings of rejection by parent(s)
- Distractibility
- Forgetfulness

- Academic difficulties
- Fantasies about their parents reuniting
- Excessive anger and hostility
- Feelings of abandonment

Adolescents may experience the following reactions:

- Depressed feelings
- Suicidal ideation
- Loneliness
- Excessive aggressive behavior
- Eating and/or sleeping difficulty
- Worry about the financial status of the family
- Risk-taking behavior including sexual and/or drug experimentation
- Withdrawal or isolative behavior
- Academic difficulties
- Concentration problems

Strategies for Assisting Students Experiencing a Divorce

School support staff can play a very helpful role in assisting students adjust to the divorce process. By meeting with students individually or in small groups (i.e., with other similar-aged peers also going through the divorce process), school psychologists, social workers, and/or guidance counselors can make a difference for children. It will be useful for children to address through discussion, drawings, art work and the like feelings that may be associated with their parents' divorce. Discussion of the fears, anxieties, guilt feelings as well as possible somatic reactions including sleep and eating problems may help children to realize that what they are experiencing is very "normal" under the unusual circumstances. Coping and relaxation strategies can also be explored.

Teachers should work with support personnel and be apprised of the emotional and cognitive status of the child. Academic demands may need to be lessened or modified temporarily. Signs and symptoms that the student may encounter should be discussed with teaching staff. **Teachers have a beneficial vantage point as they see the child on a daily basis and monitor their interactions with peers and other adults**.

Parent conferences can be helpful as an adjunct to counseling and support at school. Parent meetings should offer emotional and informational support to the parent which could ultimately benefit the child. Parents can be offered several suggestions to assist their child or teen at home including:

- Spend more quality time with the child or children
- Convey a sense of safety and security

- Encourage the child to talk without insisting on expression
- Encourage outside school activities
- Respect the child and his or her privacy
- Do not involve the child in arguments or disputes
- Have and maintain household rules
- Attempt to keep the child's daily routine simple and predictable
- Offer extra-help or tutoring for extra academic help (if needed)
- Provide close monitoring, especially if you suspect risky behavior (primarily for adolescents)
- Keep communication open and encourage family discussions
- Allow the child to remain a child (i.e., do not use them as a "spouse replacement")
- Do not expect the child to make the adjustment quickly
- Be patient when the child asks questions, especially about the other parent
- Give reassurance to the child that he or she is loved

Helping and nurturing a child's strengths and resiliency will foster a return to more adaptive functioning. However, other factors that can complicate the divorce process include difficulties with child support that may ensue, physical and/or verbal violence in the home between family members and custody disputes. In such cases, professional counseling outside of the school should be recommended to parents. Collaboration between outside support services and school staff is suggested with confidentiality maintained as a high priority.

> **Motor vehicle accidents are the leading cause of death for 15 to 20 year old individuals.**

VII. Working with Student Survivors of Motor Vehicle Accidents

Involvement with motor vehicle accidents is an unfortunate but common experience in the United States among adolescents. In fact, motor vehicle accidents are the leading cause of death for 15 to 20 year old individuals. In 2000, 3,594 drivers 15 to 20 years old were killed with an additional 348,000 injured in such crashes (NHTSA, 2000). Of all the drivers involved in fatal crashes in 2000, 14% were drivers between 15 and 20 years of age (NHTSA, 2000). In addition to the physical difficulties encountered by survivors, emotional and cognitive problems are also commonly produced by an automobile accident.

Presentation of the Student Survivor of a Motor Vehicle Accident

The impact that a car accident has on the student will vary considerably from individual to individual and may vary with the age of the student. Vehicular accidents have the potential to leave people feeling powerlessness and vulnerable. Moreover, such students are at risk of developing numerous acute stress reactions (Matsakis, 1996). Some of these symptoms may be manifested as the following, depending on the age of the student:

Preschool and Elementary Age Students:

- sadness & crying
- school avoidance
- physical complaints (e.g., headaches)
- poor concentration
- irritability
- fear of personal harm
- regressive behavior (clinging, whining)
- nightmares
- anxiety and excessive fears
- confusion
- eating difficulty
- withdrawal
- repetitive play (e.g., crashing objects)

Adolescent Students:

- sleep disturbance
- withdrawal
- eating problems
- loss of interest in activities
- rebelliousness/acting-out behavior
- anxiety
- fear of personal harm
- physical pain
- poor school performance
- depression
- concentration difficulties
- survivor guilt
- Intrusive recollections of the accident
- fears of cars and driving
- exaggerated startle response
- difficulty driving or being near the accident site
- apathy
- aggressive behavior and anger
- agitation or decrease in energy level

Strategies for Assisting Student Survivors of a Motor Vehicle Accident

Interview with the student who was involved in the motor vehicle accident by school staff should be considered (if the individual is amenable and/or physically able). Blanchard and Hickling (1997) have indicated that there are several variables that should be considered when trying to assist survivors. These include:

- Is the individual having re-experiencing symptoms including intrusive recollections, nightmares, flashbacks or distress when reminded of the accident?

- Is the person actively trying to avoid thoughts or reminders of the accident?

- How serious were the physical injuries?

- Was the individual brought to an emergency room and/or hospitalized?

- How frightened or horrified was the individual regarding the possibility of dying?

- Does the individual have a history of prior psychopathology (e.g., depression, anxiety)?

- Does the individual have a history of prior traumatization?

- Was anyone killed in the accident?

It has been estimated that over 35% of individuals involved in a motor vehicle accident may develop Posttraumatic Stress Disorder (Blanchard and Hickling, 1997). Providing a supportive recovery environment at school and recommending such support for parents are essential. Students and parents or guardians should be educated about the signs and symptoms of traumatic stress typically experienced by survivors of accidents. Students should never be told to "get over it already" or "it was just a car accident." They should know that what they are feeling are *normal* reactions to an *abnormal* event.

Modification of academic instruction may be necessary. Extra academic support or tutoring can be helpful if academic deterioration is observed. In-school counseling (individual or small group) may be indicated. Coping strategies to consider using include deep breathing exercises, journalizing, art and drawing, poetry writing, exercise and listening to music. It is important to consider that some students will have a "delayed-onset" of traumatic symptoms, perhaps, weeks or months following the accident. If decompensation is noted (i.e., there is a progressive worsening of symptoms or symptoms do not seem to be improving in the weeks following the accident), professional counseling and/or psychiatric consultation outside of school is strongly recommended.

CHAPTER EIGHT

A Perspective on Preventing School Violence

Not long ago the most severe problems encountered in our schools were students running in the halls, making excessive noise, cutting a line, talking out-of-turn, chewing gum or violating a dress code.

Today, we are faced with an increase in violence including assaults and gang activity. We are seeing an increase in the frequency of substance abuse, self-mutilation, suicide, abandonment of newborn babies, and serious injuries and deaths from automobile accidents. We are also contending with new types of violence including terrorist attacks, hostage-taking, snipers, murders, "hit lists," threatening graffiti, bomb scares and real bombs.

In this chapter, a perspective on how we may *prevent* school violence is offered.

What are the causes of school-based violence?

A wide spectrum of traumatic events are impacting our Nation's schools. Consequently, our school systems are being charged with the responsibility of responding to school-based crises. In recent years, school districts have been scrambling to develop comprehensive crisis response plans. **We no longer question if a school will be faced with a tragedy, but when.**

Many factors contribute to the causes of school violence. Research is helping us to understand the relationship between violent television programs, movies, music lyrics and violent behavior. Additionally, the interactive nature of violent computer and video games is being investigated.

We hear about the availability of guns and other weapons and we cannot ignore the data. During the last decade, nearly 80% of all violent deaths in schools were caused by guns (The Center for the Study and Prevention of Violence, 1999).

There is a dramatic increase in alcohol and substance use among our children, peer pressure and gang involvement. We are learning about children who are tormented and teased, and then go on to harm themselves and others. We are seeing the effects of divorce, "latchkey kids," parents working long hours and an absence of parental supervision, training and example-setting. Today, there are relaxed curfews, a lack of respect for authority and a lack of family involvement with schools. There is a changing family structure as well, with a large number of single parent families, grandparents and extended family living in the home.

Today, there is a growing trend of violence related to race and/or religion. This is particularly disturbing in light of the fact that diversity in America is rapidly increasing. The extent to which these variables are related to the quantitative and qualitative changes in violent school-based crises will become more apparent with time and with further empirical investigation.

The inevitability of illness, accidents and loss may be accepted and even anticipated by schools that often view themselves as microcosms of our world. But why is there such a dramatic increase in deliberately-caused tragedies—those of intentional human design?

At the very core of our problem is a *fundamental communication breakdown in families*—the result, in large part, of an increasingly technological and mechanized world. We are spending less time communicating, teaching and modeling appropriate behavior with our children—we are losing the battle to the proliferation of electronic media in a rapidly changing, mechanized world (Lerner, 1999).

At the very core of our problem is a fundamental communication breakdown in families— the result, in large part, of an increasingly technological and mechanized world.

At the breakfast table, printed and televised media offer a daily dose of violence. And today, our children leave or avoid the dinner table or family room, opting for the new era in violent television, video and computer games, and Internet chat rooms. Consequently, our children lack interpersonal communication, coping and problem-solving skills to meet the challenges of our new world— one reason why an increasing number of them act-out feelings of anger and frustration in dangerous attention-seeking ways, "self-medicate" with alcohol and other substances, and commit suicide at a higher rate than ever before.

How can we prevent school violence?

Today, our school systems are investing in expanded security forces, the installation of metal detectors and surveillance cameras, hand-held communication devices, "panic buttons," and computer "fire walls." Safety audits are becoming standard operating procedure. Although there are certainly benefits gained from taking these mechanical steps, we must address the root of the problem.

We need to help our children and adolescents to develop and enhance their communication and problem-solving skills. We must teach them how to actively listen and to empathize when relating with others. We must help our children to understand the importance of articulating their feelings about themselves and for others, and to know that it is okay to err on the side of caution when expressing concerns about others. We must regularly remind them that they can turn to their parents and/or school support personnel who will take the time to listen and respond to them We must invest in the development of people skills (Lerner, 1999).

Far too often our children hear of disturbing ideation or plans prior to a tragedy and they do not know how to respond. It is not until the aftermath of a disaster that we see survivors interviewed and we hear them describe how the perpetrator had, in some way, suggested impending doom. In cases of adolescent suicide, more than 80% of kids who commit suicide tell someone, in some way, that they are going to end their life. Our children do not know what to do or where to turn with critical information.

We must work toward improving communication, through a multimodal approach, in order to prevent violent school tragedies. We can address emotional, cognitive, social, behavioral and physiological factors. For instance, we can help our children and adolescents to identify physiological changes in their bodies which may precede or coincide with feelings of frustration and anger. We can help them to understand which of their behaviors/actions cause others to become frustrated and angry. We can teach them to become aware of and to identify negative self-statements—cognitions that generate feelings of frustration and anger. And, we can help our children to learn to replace self-defeating statements with positive coping statements. Behaviorally, we can model and espouse appropriate moral behavior, set limits and be consistent with our behavior. Ultimately, we can teach our children to show compassion and sincerity in relating with others.

We must help our children to understand that conflict is a natural part of interpersonal relationships. When we handle conflict well it presents an opportunity to learn, to better understand ourselves and to generate creative solutions. When we handle conflict poorly, it can lead to violence.

We must help our children to make more adaptive, goal-directed decisions when faced with feelings of frustration. For example, we can teach them that it is okay to walk away from altercations or to take a few moments to "cool down." We can teach our children to express themselves assertively, to implement relaxation techniques, and to utilize conflict resolution and peer mediation skills. Interestingly, when we ask children and adolescents what they believe may help to reduce the frequency of school-based tragedies, they indicate that there needs to be more constructive opportunities for expression of feelings. On the other hand, we must keep in mind that conflict resolution techniques and peer mediation programs presuppose conflict.

We must reach our children when they are very young and invest in developing communication and problem-solving skills.

How can we prevent school violence? We must reach our children when they are very young and invest in developing communication and problem-solving skills.

Today, we must view all members of the school family as being "at risk." However, there are "early warning signs" to identify individuals who may be at greater risk for engaging in violent behavior (see Practical Document E). Let us all become hypervigilant, learn to err on the side of caution, and work toward preventing violent tragedies in our schools.

CHAPTER NINE

Managing Disturbing Threats in Our Schools

Inevitably, crises occur on school campuses. Such events are typically unexpected and have the potential to leave a school building and/or district feeling violated and at times, overwhelmed. Disturbing threats, however, do not necessarily mean that a traumatic event will ensue. Threats of violence, hit lists, threatening graffiti, intimidating e-mail or internet postings, and intruder threats are all examples of incidents that are distressing for school systems and require efficient response to prevent the escalation of fear and worry that may result. Schools must have plans in place to address and ultimately, resolve any upset that such an event may produce. **A structured, pre-planned response that includes a trained team of staff members can help return a school back to its pre-crisis functioning level.**

Specific threats should always raise concerns for a school district. When a threat is made that is associated with killing or hurting individuals, has to do with something potentially harmful or hazardous or is made by an individual or individuals with known access to a weapons, firearms, bomb-making material, etc., an appropriate plan must be in place. It has been reported that the more *specific* and *lethal* the threat (e.g., "a bomb will detonate at 2:00 PM in the Principal's office") and the more follow-up calls received, the greater the cause for concern.

An Overview of the Problem

Approximately 100 bombs are set off in schools every year. Many more threats of violence or intimidating acts are encountered in over 90,000 schools in the United States. In New York State alone, for the 1999-2000 school year, over 500 threats including bomb, arson and anthrax threats, were reported. A school district in Maryland had more than 150 bomb threats in one year and over 50 related arrests. Although there is no one answer to explain why individuals make threats of violence or act to intimidate others, especially in the school setting, many believe that it is related to:

- a need for attention from others,
- a sense of alienation or detachment from friends and family,
- contagion effects or "copycat" effects from media coverage, and
- need for avenge or perceived wrong or injustice.

Identification of individuals who may engage in such acts is a difficult task. There is no evidence to support that "profiling" of such individuals is useful because no one trait or set of traits can reliably distinguish a school bomber from the perpetrator of an intimidating e-mail threat or arsonist.

Preventative Measures

In order to maintain a safe school environment, schools should remain pro-active in their approach to crisis management. This includes the development and maintenance of multidisciplinary school crisis response teams, education regarding violence prevention and crisis prevention for administrators, staff and students, a well-defined communication system at all levels of the school district, and a physically safe school building. Some related suggestions to facilitate a safer learning environment include:

- keep adequate lighting in all hallways,
- have caller I.D. installed on phones,
- use the same telephone system across the entire school district to facilitate the tracing of calls,
- use a public address system that reaches all points in the buildings,
- have a mechanism to communicate with portable classrooms, playgrounds, etc.,
- close off unused stairways,
- maintain an alarm system and closed-circuit monitoring system,
- limit roof and basement access,
- monitor of student and faculty parking lots (especially, at the secondary level),
- keep a list of staff members who have keyed access to the building,
- determine a designated spokesperson for the district,
- use I.D. badges with picture for all staff and faculty,
- maintain current student I.D.s,
- prepare a list of emergency telephone numbers,
- establish a hot-line for information and rumor management,
- conduct safety and/or evacuation drills,
- maintain working relationship with local law enforcement and emergency response officials,
- conduct thorough background check on anyone applying to work in the school,
- provide pre-emptive counseling for students (and staff) including anger management training, social skills training and conflict mediation instruction, and
- offer school or community-based activities for students during non-school days, weekends or vacations.

Crisis Response

With regard to an efficient emergency response, the following suggestions may be most useful:

- have a clear emergency signal that differs depending on the type of emergency (e.g., one bell indicates a bomb evacuation will occur),
- identify who can declare an emergency and under what conditions,
- make floor plans and evacuation routes readily accessible,
- know the location of utility shut-off for gas, power and water,
- maintain phone/e-mail lists for emergency response agencies/hospitals,
- keep up-to-date phone lists for staff, parent organizations or volunteers,
- maintain an emergency kit in every classroom that includes: class rosters, basic office supplies, emergency telephone numbers for every student, bandages, plastic/latex gloves, rain protection tarp, triage tags for students' names, record-keeping materials (i.e., to identify whom students are released to), laminated sign on a stick with teacher's name, candy and gum, playing cards, frisbee, plastic cups, toilet paper, blankets, safety pins, first-aid kit, sunscreen, waterless soap, duct tape, permanent markers, baby wipes,
- develop a plan and train staff members to respond in a standardized fashion with regard to locking of classroom doors and windows or movement from the classroom around school grounds,
- establish a common area for unsupervised children to assemble,
- establish a protocol for identifying safe and injured students,
- designate a location for parents to meet their children,
- establish a buddy system for all students,
- designate a place for news media to gather,
- assign a specific administrator to assist special education students and staff as well as students with limited English proficiency, and
- review and update emergency plans regularly.

In an effort to effectively respond to disturbing threats, school districts should not wait for a crisis to occur in order to develop response plans. Having a plan in place for a variety of situations is recommended. The following outline is intended to provide valuable information and suggestions regarding the handling of a variety of *specific* threats that a school system may encounter.

Practical Suggestions for Responding to Bomb Threats

Many bomb threats are called in to a target or message recipient. Threats can be made directly on the telephone, through written communication or recording. The caller may offer knowledge of where the explosive device is or will be placed. Also, a caller may want to create an atmosphere of panic and disrupt the equilibrium of a school setting. The following, at the very least, should be considered in response to such a threat:

- Remain calm and do not hang up on the caller even if the call is over.
- Be careful who is informed of the threat because rumors and panic may easily spread.
- When received over the telephone, the person taking the message should attempt to keep the caller on the phone as long as possible.
- Take written notes. Be sure to include: time/date of call, suspected age, gender, and race of caller, exactly what the caller said, unique qualities about the caller's voice, emotional state of caller, background noises, phone number of caller (assuming the call is not blocked and you have Caller ID). Note the use of any threatening language (e.g., foul, irrational, incoherent).
- Notify Central and Building Administration immediately.
- Consult with local law enforcement agency.
- Determine if or how a search of the building and grounds will be conducted. For example, this may range from a low profile search of the exterior grounds to a more comprehensive search involving staff searching their respective work areas to a search with partial evacuation and ultimately, an evacuation of the entire building.
- Searches typically begin on the exterior of the school building and move inward. Efficient searches proceed from the lower level to the upper levels of the building with search personnel working toward each other.
- The decision to evacuate should be based on objective evaluation (e.g., specifics of threat, etc.). If an evacuation is to occur, proceed in an orderly fashion taking into account how and when students will be released. A pre-planned evacuation procedure should be followed. Assure that everyone leaving the building is accounted for at a pre-designated location.
- If evacuation does occur, ensure that all students, faculty and staff are at least 1000 to 3000 feet away from the building.
- Never use elevators to evacuate.
- Do not use walkie-talkie type radios which can detonate electronic devices and activate a bomb.
- Unusual or suspected objects should be reported immediately to administration and never touched or moved.
- Consider all bomb threats to be valid until reasonable precautions have been taken.
- Upon resolution, provide debriefing and counseling.
- Follow-up with students, faculty, and parents.
- Follow-up with faculty meeting, parent letters and/or forum.

Practical Suggestions for Responding to Intimidating Graffiti

Graffiti is a crime. All states have vandalism laws regarding graffiti. Threatening or intimidating graffiti has the potential to initiate rumors and spread fear on a school campus. The following suggestions may facilitate the response:

- Notify the Principal immediately.
- Contact local law enforcement.
- Take photographs of the graffiti, preferably with a Polaroid or other instant camera to avoid delays in processing.
- Complete an incident report.
- Keep a log documenting the location of the graffiti and how, when, and by whom it was discovered.
- Cover the graffiti with plastic or cloth until the police approve its removal.
- Remove the graffiti upon consent of law enforcement.
- Hold faculty meeting, if appropriate.
- Use a telephone tip-line to provide a safe means for students or community members to report information regarding the incident anonymously.
- Follow discipline process, if perpetrator(s) is/are known.
- Provide debriefing, discussion and counseling, as needed.

Practical Suggestions for Responding to Intruder Threats

When a stranger enters a school building with the intent to intimidate, threaten or attack, a school system must have a protocol to respond expeditiously. As always, practice drills should always occur prior to the onset of a crisis situation. The following suggestions may facilitate the response:

- Assess the severity of the situation and determine the safest action for students, staff, and faculty.
- Do not set off building alarms. This could irritate the intruder or put people in harm's way.
- Notify Building Security.
- Call 911.
- Determine whether students should remain in their classroom or evacuate the building. Students and faculty should not move from their setting (e.g., classroom) unless otherwise notified.
- If an evacuation is to occur, proceed in an orderly fashion taking into account how and when students will be released. A pre-planned evacuation procedure should be followed. Assure that everyone leaving the building is accounted for at a pre-designated location.
- If the building is evacuated, no one should re-enter unless given proper authorization.

- Contact school district administration.
- Remain calm and attempt to isolate and/or negotiate with the perpetrator, if it seems appropriate. Avoid confrontation, especially with an armed intruder.
- Listen closely to the direction of law enforcement officials.
- Secure medical attention if anyone is injured.
- Determine who will handle press/media
- Designate how traffic and crowd control will be handled.
- Upon resolution, provide debriefing and counseling.
- Follow-up with students, faculty, and parents.
- Follow-up with faculty meeting, parent forum, etc.

Practical Suggestions for Responding to E-Mail Threats

Electronically sent threatening mail via computer has increasingly become a cause for concern within school districts. Whether a threat is e-mailed from an individual's home or from within a school building, is something that local law enforcement would have to determine. However, all threats should be taken seriously. The following suggestions may facilitate the response:

- Inform Building Principal.
- Inform District Administration.
- Always print the threat or related material from the computer to show authorities.
- Do not delete items from the computer. Oftentimes, identifying information is sent with e-mail correspondence. This will be useful data for investigators to review.
- Notify local law enforcement.
- Use a telephone tip-line to provide a safe means for students or community members to report information regarding the incident anonymously.
- If the e-mail is directed at a particular individual or group, appropriate notification and support should be provided to that person or group of individuals. Notification should be made to parents/guardians as well. Offer parent meeting if it seems warranted.
- Provide debriefing and counseling, if needed.

Conclusion

In an effort to provided an environment that is safe and conducive to education, school systems need to assess and refine response plans on an ongoing basis. Because threatening events are typically unexpected, they have the potential to leave a school building and/or district feeling violated and overwhelmed. Comprehensive crisis management is not only designed to prevent such incidents, but always considers the school district's response *during* and *after* the event.

Consequently, a multidisciplinary crisis response team should be in place and available for students and staff quickly to provide debriefing and counseling for any resulting trauma. The provision and dissemination of information regarding the event should be conducted with discretion. As always, the building principal or superintendent should work closely with local law enforcement and/or emergency services personnel to provide an effective and quick resolution to the situation and return a school back to its pre-crisis functioning level.

CHAPTER TEN

A Theoretical Perspective on Preventing Disturbing Threats

A pattern has emerged. In the aftermath of highly publicized tragedies in our nation's schools, we experience a dramatic increase in the frequency of disturbing threats—bomb scares, "hit lists" and threatening graffiti. Following is a theoretical perspective on reducing the frequency of disturbing threats in our schools (Lerner, 1999).

When a bomb threat is telephoned, e-mailed or written on a bathroom wall, there is an enormous impact on the school community. The potential need to evacuate a school building under such circumstances presents a host of complex decisions for school administrators. Ultimately, ensuring the safety of the school family and preventing further disruption of the educational process is crucial.

Beyond bomb scares, there are other disturbing threats, such as "hit lists" and threatening graffiti. For example, the traumatic stress endured by fourteen students, teachers and school administrators named on a poster placed in the entrance area of one high school was profound. The poster described how each of them would be harmed. Furthermore, the fear that was experienced by another school family after the statement "Everyone will die on June 4th" had a far-reaching impact upon the entire community. After the building principal informed parents of the threat, nearly all of the sixteen hundred students were absent from school—many roamed the streets of the community.

Understanding what causes or contributes to the surge of disturbing threats in our schools in the wake of well-publicized tragedies may help to mitigate similar behavior. The reasons why some students choose to make bomb threats, develop "hit lists," or write threatening graffiti are complex. Ultimately, empirical research will help us to understand the relationship between these threats and such variables as domestic violence, sexual abuse, substance abuse, chronic teasing and tormenting, etc. Notwithstanding, we need a strategy now. Following is a theoretical perspective based upon years of experience in working with children and adolescents as well as an interpretation of extant literature.

There are a significant number of young people who are feeling alone and powerless in our rapidly changing world. When these individuals observe the tremendous and overwhelming attention following highly-publicized dramatic events, many of them identify with the aggressor(s). They may fantasize about an opportunity to overcome feelings of aloneness, inadequacy, weakness and powerlessness. They envision themselves acting-out and perhaps overcompensate for these dystonic feelings. Fortunately, relatively few act upon these violent impulses with significant magnitude. Apparently there is some impulse control which prevents them from going to the extent that perpetrators of rampage killings ultimately manifest. However, in their minds, they see an opportunity to take action, of a lesser magnitude, and still draw a great deal of attention.

Why do some schools experience many threats? Why do others experience few? And, why do others seem to escape such experiences? Perhaps the climate established by the school staff and administration is directly related to the frequency of disturbing threats.

Educators must be careful not to challenge disturbed young people with statements like, "Our school is a safe place and we will not experience the kinds of events that you heard about yesterday...." Such statements may serve to create a "double bind"—a challenge for these individuals. They may incite these students to try to disprove authority figures, to make themselves feel more powerful and to help them to compensate for their feelings of inadequacy and weakness.

Furthermore, educators that ignore highly-publicized tragedies occurring in our nation's schools are missing a critical opportunity to help young people to articulate disturbing thoughts and feelings, and to learn adaptive coping strategies. When bad things happen, we need to talk and be there for each other. During times of crisis, we learn to appreciate the value of empathic communication.

What can we do to decrease the frequency of disturbing threats? If indeed the "type" of individual or individuals who generate threats are trying to overcompensate for feelings of aloneness, inadequacy, weakness and powerlessness, we must work toward helping these young people to understand that the effect that they are trying to achieve by making a threat (i.e., to overcompensate for these disturbing feelings) will not result in the attainment of their perceived goal (e.g., to feel more powerful). Rather, the result of the threat may likely cause them to be arrested, feel very alone while incarcerated, more inadequate, weaker and truly powerless. If in fact we focus our attention on helping young people to understand and observe the CONSEQUENCES of being caught for making disturbing threats, the frequency of such threats may be dramatically reduced.

How can we focus our attention on the consequences of making disturbing threats? The responsibility here lies at a number of levels. Within the school, talk through scenarios. For example, "Imagine if police officers were racing to a school and one struck and killed a 26 year-old mother. How would you feel if you had telephoned-in a threat?" Schools can also focus on the consequence of disturbing threats by stating policies. For example, "Individuals who are caught will face expulsion. This means that...." Schools can additionally establish clear policies whereby all "lost time" due to disturbing threats would have to be made up. Outside of the schools, legislation could be enacted that would make bomb threats a felony in all states. Parents could be held financially responsible for the municipal costs of responding to threats. The media could show alleged perpetrators being led in handcuffs to police vehicles, rather than show photographs of adolescent killers sitting and smiling with their "peers."

We can take steps to help young people to understand the consequences of disturbing threats by focusing attention not on the glorification of such acts, but on the reality of their actions.

CHAPTER ELEVEN

Helping Ourselves in the Aftermath of a School-Based Crisis

Most educators do not enter the profession expecting to help students and staff respond in the face of a tragedy. However, in reality, when a school-based crisis presents, meeting the needs of the school family calls for the collaborative effort of *all* educators. This chapter looks beyond strategies for helping others and, instead, describes how we may help *ourselves* in the wake of a tragedy.

Working with students and staff who are in acute emotional distress requires an intensity that is both mental and physical. **Realize that you may likely be exposed to the very event that you are called upon to help others.** It is imperative that you consider your own state of mind prior to engaging in the provision of **Acute Traumatic Stress Management** (see Chapter 4) and school crisis response protocol. If you are overwhelmed by the situation, or if you are currently experiencing a time of emotional distress in your life, it would be wise to have another individual provide help for others. Following is a list of strategies that you may utilize in managing your *own* responses during a crisis and in its immediate aftermath. These strategies may also be shared with individuals with whom you are helping (Lerner and Shelton, 2001).

During the Event

- Become aware of and monitor *your* emotional, cognitive, behavioral and physiological reactions. Consider the effect the event is having on you. Acknowledge to yourself that your involvement is creating these reactions.

- If you find that the discussion is causing you to react physically (i.e., rapid heart rate, breathing increase, sweating, etc.) take a slow deep breath and tell yourself to relax—take a second deep breath and relax. If you are finding the event overwhelming, and it is possible, separate and share your feelings with a colleague.

- Realize that acute traumatic stress may compromise your ability to make good decisions and can therefore place you in danger. If you find that you are unable to concentrate, focus on the individual and the specific words they are saying—work to actively listen to what they are communicating. Slow down the conversation and try repeating what you have just heard.

- Acknowledge and speak of the impact the event is having on you as a human being. For example following the sudden death of a beloved teacher, you might say, "This is really tough for all of us...." However, make every effort to avoid self-disclosure of specific, personal information with others (e.g., "I remember during my first year of teaching when another teacher was killed in a car accident...."). **Remember that it is OK not to be OK, and that displaying your emotions can reinforce for victims your genuine concern** (Lerner and Shelton, 2001).

Following the Event

- Acknowledge that the event itself and the connections you have established with others can have a lasting impact on you. Words people have spoken and the emotions they displayed may become imprinted in *your* mind.

- Reflect upon what has just occurred. Maintain an *awareness* of your emotional, cognitive, behavioral and physiological reactions. Find a trusted friend to talk to about your experience. Remember to keep in confidence what people shared with you. Talk about *your* reactions to the experience. Sharing the experience will help you to assimilate what has occurred.

- Realize that repetitive thoughts and sleep difficulties are normal reactions. Do not fight the sleep difficulty, this will usually pass in a few days. Try the following. Eliminate caffeine for four hours prior to your bedtime, create the best sleep environment you can, consider taking a few moments before turning out the lights to write down your thoughts, thus emptying your mind. Try reading or listening to peaceful music.

- Avoid excessive media exposure. Particularly during highly-publicized tragedies. This was certainly a problem in the wake of the September 11 tragedy. Take time to get away from the action.

- Give yourself permission to rest, relax and engage in some non-threatening activity. Engage in physical exercise to dissipate the stress energy that has been generated.

- Spend time with your family, friends and your spiritual leader; stay connected with them. Resist the urge to retreat into your own world. You need their support following an emotionally-charged event.

- Create a journal. Writing about traumatic experiences is helpful in exposing ourselves to painful thoughts and feelings, and in helping us to assimilate these experiences.

- If necessary, seek the assistance of a professional. If you find that the experience is powerful and is staying with you for an extended period of time, allow yourself the advantage of professional support and education. Remember that you are a normal person who has experienced an abnormal event.

- Have the strength to let go. It requires courage to face the powerful emotions within you (Lerner and Shelton, 2001).

Conclusion

In our efforts to help others during traumatic events, we can fall prey to traumatic stress. Additionally, within the school environment, *we* may likely be struggling with feelings of loss and sadness. It is critical that we recognize when it is appropriate for us to intervene with others and when we should leave this responsibility to another caregiver. If we do elect to provide support to others, we must always remember to take care of ourselves.

CHAPTER TWELVE

Practical Documents

A. School Crisis Response: A Practical Checklist

The following checklist was developed to facilitate an effective crisis response *during,* and in the aftermath of, a school-based crisis. This list will require modification to address the nature of the crisis situation and should not take the place of competent professional services. By reaching our school families early, we can potentially prevent the *acute* stress reactions of today from becoming the *chronic* stress disorders of tomorrow (Lerner, 1997).

I. Fact Gathering
❑ Notify building principal
❑ Clarify facts surrounding the crisis
❑ Contact school district administration
❑ Contact parents/guardians (of individuals involved/affected)
  • Obtain consent for release of information
❑ Contact police and/or fire department
❑ Principal consults with assistant principal and/or school psychologist
❑ Determine the need for assembling the Crisis Response Team

II. The Call to Action
❑ Assemble the Crisis Response Team
❑ Share facts with team members and assess the impact of the crisis
  • When did the event occur (e.g., during a lunch period, over the summer)?
  • Where did the event occur (e.g., on school grounds)?
  • How did it happen (e.g., accidental, intentional, expected)?
  • How many students and staff are affected by the event?
  • Which students and staff are affected?
  • How are the students and staff affected?
  • How are the faculty responding?
  • Should classes be suspended temporarily or assignments altered?
  • Should students be released from school?
  • How are students indirectly being affected (e.g., siblings/friends at other buildings in the district, etc.)?
❑ Determine if additional support services are needed (e.g., psychologists/social workers/ counselors from other buildings)
  • Weigh efficacy of "unknown" professionals
  • Provide identification badges for these outside professionals
❑ Update school district administration

III. Notification Procedures
❑ Consider:
  • Announcement to students and faculty
  • Announcement should not give too many details that could be misinterpreted
  • A student assembly
  • Location of support personnel (e.g., library)
  • Need for students to sign out of class and in with support personnel
  • Mailbox memorandum to faculty and staff
  • Emergency faculty meeting (first thing in the morning)
  • Notification of students in classrooms by Crisis Response Team

IV. Crisis Response Team in Motion
- ❏ Administrators and security circulate through the building.
  - • "Pockets" of grieving students should be directed to location of support personnel
- ❏ Consider letter to be sent to students' homes — facts, summary, reactions, guidelines, contact numbers.
- ❏ All staff can utilize the *Acute Traumatic Stress Management* model.
  - • "Connect, Ground, Support, Normalize and Prepare"
- ❏ Team members should visit selected classrooms to provide opportunity for discussion.
- ❏ Teachers should allow opportunity for students to ventilate.
- ❏ Counseling with individuals and small groups by psychologists, social workers and/or guidance counselors.
  - • Attempt to cultivate a "helping relationship" characterized by empathy, warmth and genuineness.
  - • Encourage people to express their feelings.
  - • Be careful not to lecture and allow periods of silence.
  - • Avoid cliches such as, "Be strong..." and "You're doing so well..."
    Such cliches may only serve to reinforce an individual's feelings of aloneness.
  - • Attempt to "normalize" grief reactions.
  - • Remember that cultural differences exist in the overt expression of emotions.
  - • Maintaining confidentiality, when possible, is crucial.
  - • Provide snacks (e.g., juice, cookies, etc.) to students and support staff.
  - • It is important to remember that *we* have support while helping others during this difficult time.

- ❏ Identify high risk individuals.
- ❏ Contact parents/guardians of high risk students.
- ❏ Provide referrals for outside support (if indicated).
- ❏ Provide hot-line numbers to parents/guardians for after school hours (if necessary).
- ❏ Carefully document events.
- ❏ Consider open forum for parents (after school hours).
- ❏ Schedule follow-up by support personnel for high risk individuals.
- ❏ Schedule faculty meeting.
- ❏ Remain sensitive to how team members are being perceived.

V. Addressing the Media
- ❏ Develop a response - consider confidentiality, family wishes, liability of erroneous information.
- ❏ Designate a spokesperson - "no one else talks."
- ❏ Designate alternate spokesperson.

VI. Debriefing
- ❏ Review the events of the day.
- ❏ Revise the intervention strategies (e.g., plan for upcoming days).
- ❏ Monitor reactions of crisis team members - "compassion fatigue."

VII. Funeral
- ❏ Consider the wishes of the students' family.
- ❏ Consider the wishes of the victim(s) family regarding attendance.
- ❏ Consider the age of the attendants.
- ❏ Consider the number of staff attending.
- ❏ Have support personnel available there.

VIII. Memorialization
- ❏ Consider appropriateness.
- ❏ Consider a method:
  - • a moment of silence
  - • a plaque
  - • planting a tree
  - • a dedication
  - • flying the school flag at half-mast

SCHOOL CRISIS RESPONSE: A PRACTICAL CHECKLIST

B. Practical Suggestions for Assisting Children in the Aftermath of a Tragedy

Reprinted from *A Practical Guide for Crisis Response in Our Schools*
© 2003 by The American Academy of Experts in Traumatic Stress—Reproduced with Permission
368 Veterans Memorial Highway, Commack New York 11725
Tel. (631) 543-2217 • Fax (631) 543-6977 • www.aaets.org • www.schoolcrisisresponse.com

The manner in which children react to tragic events is dependent upon a number of variables including the age of the child, personal history, personality variables, the severity and proximity of the event, level of social support available and the type and quality of intervention. It is important to realize that most children will recover from the effects of a crisis with appropriate support from family, friends, and school personnel.

It is essential that adults balance their efforts to address their child's emotional needs with their own emotional responses during times of crises. Caregivers should remain aware that in order to "be there" for children, they need to "be there" for themselves as well. Seeking professional assistance is recommended if you or your child's reactions begin to significantly interfere with life functioning or if negative emotional, cognitive, behavioral and physiological responses become predominant. The following are suggestions that you can utilize in your effort to assist children.

1. Be aware of your own reactions to the event. Very young children (e.g., preschool) take their cues regarding how to respond by monitoring the reactions of significant adults in their environment (e.g., parents, teachers, older siblings). Attempt to model calm behavior. Moreover, do not be critical of clingy behavior or other regressive reactions (e.g., nightmares, bed-wetting, somatic complaints) exhibited by the child. These are typically "normal" responses for children under significant forms of stress.

2. Keep yourself available for providing extra attention to your child. Such attention not only provides an opportunity for a child to express what they have experienced but also reaffirms their sense of closeness and security with you. Give them additional affection in the form of hugs or other physical contact if it seems appropriate. Don't avoid discussion about this incident if your child expresses a desire to talk. Assisting children *during* such a crisis when they are most vulnerable to the deleterious effects of traumatic exposure, may provide a tremendous opportunity for caregivers to stimulate healthy, adaptive functioning. Maintain a warm, genuine and facilitative or helping attitudinal climate.

3. Be mindful of the child's cognitive and emotional functioning level. Giving too much information to a younger child may foster a sense of confusion as well as fear and insecurity. Younger children require the use of simpler words and concepts. Do not be overintellectual in your effort to describe the incident (something that is easy to do as we attempt to reduce our own anxiety when discussing certain issues). Adolescents may try to minimize or downplay their concerns about the situation. Keep an open line of communication with them. Encourage, but *do not insist* on, discussion.

4. Use empathic communication by acknowledging, understanding and expressing an appreciation of your child's experience. Attempt to comprehend the feelings that lie beneath his words (and actions) and convey that understanding to him. For example, you may ask what he knows about the events and give him a chance to describe what he has been thinking about since the incident. Let him know that many people of all ages are also upset and that many are working together to prevent such a thing from happening again. When appropriate, express your own feelings (e.g., "I am sad about what happened as well . . . Let's talk about what you have been feeling . . . "). Not only does this help develop a child's vocabulary for expressing emotions (through modeling), but also begins the important process of validating and legitimizing their thoughts and feelings regarding the event. Reassure them that feelings of fear, sadness, anger, and guilt are "normal" reactions to an "abnormal" experience.

5. Do not speculate and give false information about what has taken place. This is especially true for older children (e.g., adolescents). Misrepresentation of facts may exacerbate false and distorted thinking (e.g., "Can I get drafted?"). Don't hesitate to admit that you do not have the answers for all that is asked. Don't dwell on the details and scope of the event, especially with young children. However, strive to separate fact from fiction.

6. Monitor exposure to media. Do not overexpose children to television and radio, especially preschool and elementary-aged children. This is certainly the case when graphic and perhaps, live programming is being broadcasted. Use alternate audio and video materials (e.g., videos, DVD, music) to distract them from live television viewing. You may also channel their feelings and curiosity into some form of helping behavior. For example, have them write a letter or draw pictures, donate clothes, or help raise money for those affected by the event.

7. Realistically provide reassurance about their safety. Assure them that steps are being taken to make their schools and community safer places to live, for example. Moreover, express that the event is very extraordinary and uncommon. Older kids may benefit from becoming engaged in the process of developing "safety" methods. For example, they can develop a list of emergency contact numbers or determine ways to increase communication with their family when they are away from home, etc. These responses may also foster a sense of empowerment. Again, keeping the age and developmental level of the child in mind is of paramount importance. Telling a child that they are entirely safe may be difficult at a time when you, personally, are not feeling secure. In fact, such information may be a distortion of reality. However, younger children (preschool age) will not comprehend the nature and intricacy of certain events (e.g., terrorist attacks) and thus, reassurance of safety may be the best and most healthy information that we can offer. Attempt to remain reasonably honest with adolescents about the impact of the disaster on your family as well as the world.

8. Consider the reactions of children with histories of past traumatic experiences, losses, or emotional disturbance (e.g., depression, anxiety). Traumatic incidents tend to dredge up maladaptive thoughts and feelings, especially with adolescents. Be observant for signs of suicide, substance abuse, severe sleeping and eating disturbance, and externalizing of angry or aggressive feelings. As mentioned earlier, do not hesitate to seek the assistance of a mental health professional within the school or community settings.

9. Make an effort to maintain a "normal" routine. This may be quite difficult, especially if you are directly affected by the incident (e.g., loss of a family member or friend). Keeping some consistency in household chores, dinner time, homework, bedtime can foster the healing and recovery process. Do not be overly rigid but attempt to approximate those routines that have become familiar and routine. This may help maintain a sense of "connectedness" to the past and help mitigate against anxiety and "fear of the unknown."

10. Monitor your own emotional status. Be aware that you may also be feeling grief, anxiety, guilt, and anger as you attempt to make sense out of the senseless. Keep in touch with close friends, family, clergy, school and mental health professionals as needed. Try to get adequate sleep and nutrition. Incorporate exercise and other enjoyable activities within your routine. Again, do not hesitate to obtain professional assistance if you or your child are in need.

C. Teacher Guidelines for Crisis Response

Reprinted from *A Practical Guide for Crisis Response in Our Schools*
© 2003 by The American Academy of Experts in Traumatic Stress—Reproduced with Permission
368 Veterans Memorial Highway, Commack New York 11725
Tel. (631) 543-2217 • Fax (631) 543-6977 • www.aaets.org • www.schoolcrisisresponse.com

What is a crisis and what is crisis response?

A crisis is a traumatic event that is typically unpredicted and overwhelming for those who experience it. This situation may be volatile in nature and, at times, may involve threat to the survival of an individual or groups of individuals. Moreover, a crisis state may result upon exposure to drastic and tragic change in an individual's environment which has become common and familiar to them. This alteration in the status quo is unwanted, frightening, and often renders a person with a sense of vulnerability and helplessness. Ultimately, with successful intervention, the equilibrium is restored between the environment and the individual's perception of their world as a safe and secure place. Examples of crises that can potentially have a large scale effect on the students, faculty and administrators in a school building or district include: an accident involving a student or faculty member, a suicide or death of a student or faculty member, severe violence (e.g., gang fight), hostage taking, fire at school or a natural disaster (e.g., hurricane).

Crisis response, as it pertains to the school environment, is a proactive, organized and well thought out plan to a crisis situation that has adversely affected many individuals in a school district, including students, faculty and administrators.

Why a Crisis Response Plan?

Research has revealed that schools are increasingly more prone to crisis situations that adversely affect large numbers of students and faculty. The rise in adolescent suicide, increased assaults on teachers, high levels of substance abuse among students and increased violence in the schools are some of the reasons cited. Research has also indicated that today's school districts need to contend with reactions to new types of trauma/disasters. For example, hostage taking, sniper attacks, murders, terrorist activities and bomb scares were almost nonexistent in the schools 30 years ago, but today occur with greater frequency. Thus, it is strongly recommended that school districts need to be prepared for a crisis situation that can potentially affect the functioning of their students, faculty and administrators. Lerner (1997) comments:

"There are two kinds of beach front homeowners on the south shore of Long Island: those who have faced serious erosion, and those who will. Similarly, there are two kinds of schools: those that have faced a serious crisis situation, and those that will."

Research has emerged over the past ten years supporting a proactive approach to a crisis, as opposed to one that is reactive in nature. Such an approach is much better in dealing effectively with a large scale crisis situation. A reactive approach is spontaneous, and not fully thought out, planned, or practiced, and can result in the response that is less effective in meeting the immediate, and possibly the long-term needs of the students, faculty and administrators.

In summary, a proactive approach to a crisis is one that is organized, planned and practiced and more likely results in a response that can have a dramatic effect on reducing the short and long-term consequences of the crisis on the individuals in a school district.

What types of behaviors/reactions can teachers expect from their students after a crisis situation has occurred?

The manner in which people react to crisis situations is dependent upon a number of variables including personal history, personality variables, severity and proximity of the event, level of social support and the type and quality of intervention. While no two people respond to situations, including crisis situations, in exactly the same manner, the following are often seen as <u>immediate</u> reactions to a significant crisis:

- shock, numbness,
- denial or inability to acknowledge the situation has occurred,
- dissociative behavior—appearing dazed, apathetic, expressing feelings of unreality,
- confusion,
- disorganization,
- difficulty making decisions, and
- suggestibility.

It is important to note that most children will recover from the effects of a crisis with adequate support from family, friends and school personnel. Their response to a crisis can be viewed as "a normal response to an abnormal situation." While the emotional effects of the crisis can be significant and can potentially influence functioning for weeks to months, most children will evidence a full recovery.

Following are descriptions of responses likely to observed in children:

- **Regression in Behavior:** Children who have been exposed to a crisis often exhibit behaviors that are similar to children younger than themselves. This is especially true of toddlers, preschool and elementary school children. They may return to behavior that was abandoned long ago (e.g., thumb sucking, bed-wetting, fears of the dark). Traumatized children may also exhibit separation anxiety, clinging to parents and resistance to leaving the parents' side. They may resist going to bed alone. Bladder and bowel control may be temporarily lost in younger children.

- **Increase in Fears and Anxiety:** Children also exhibit an increase in their fears and worries. They may again become afraid of situations they mastered long ago. As mentioned above they may become fearful of the dark and refuse to go to bed alone. A school phobia may emerge where the child refuses to go to school for fear of something happening and/or fear of leaving his/her parents. They may openly verbalize their fear of the crisis occurring again in the school. It is important that parents do not allow the child to remain home as a means to deal with his/her anxiety. This will result in the anxiety increasing once the child needs to return to school. Due to the increase in fears, additional demands are made for parent attention and support. Adolescents may experience a more generalized anxiety and not the specific types of fears that are seen in younger children.

- **Decreased Academic Performance and Poor Concentration:** Given the increase in anxiety and the disruption a crisis can have on children's sense of safety and security, there is a decrease in the amount of mental energy and focus available to learn and complete academic assignments.

- **Increased Aggression and Oppositional Behavior, and Decreased Frustration Tolerance:** Children who have been exposed to a crisis can experience difficulty controlling their anger and frustration. Situations that would not have caused a heightened emotional response prior to the crisis, can post-crisis result in an aggressive response and/or expression of frustration. Adolescents may also exhibit an increase in oppositional behavior, refusing to live by the rules and regulations of school and home, and/or meet their responsibilities (e.g., chores, academic assignments). Some adolescents may resort to antisocial behavior (e.g., stealing).

- **Increased Irritability, Emotional Liability and Depressive Feelings:** Children can also exhibit stronger and more variable emotional responses to situations. There could be symptoms of depression that include general sense of sadness, difficulty falling and remaining asleep or sleeping more than normal, change in eating habits, loss of interest in activities once enjoyed, social withdrawal, mental and physical fatigue and/or suicidal ideation. In younger children there may be an increase in irritability and moodiness.

- **Denial:** In an effort to cope with the psychological and emotional ramifications of a crisis, certain children and adolescents will deny that a crisis has occurred and/or deny the significance of a crisis. A child whose mother has died suddenly may demand that he can return home so that they can watch their favorite television program together. An adolescent whose favorite teacher was badly injured in a car accident may insist that he will recover fully, despite the medical evidence that indicates that this will not happen. Children who continue to utilize denial to cope may need to be confronted in a sensitive but straight forward manner. Anger and resentment may be expressed when confronting the child with the reality. In time, and with support, children do come to accept the reality of a situation.

Understanding the typical reactions of individuals exposed to a crisis situation is a critical step in identifying people who may be in need of further professional assistance. Several investigators (Greenstone & Levittown, 1993; Klingman, 1987; Weaver, 1995) have described **age-appropriate reactions** of individuals exposed to a traumatic event. Although there is heterogeneity in the reactions of individuals surrounding a crisis, most of these responses are expected reactions and subside in several weeks following the crisis.

Preschool Children (Ages 1 through 5)
- thumb sucking
- speech difficulties
- bed wetting
- decreases or increases in appetite
- fear of the dark
- clinging and whining
- loss of bladder control
- separation difficulties

Childhood (Ages 5 through 11)
- sadness & crying
- school avoidance
- physical complaints (e.g., headaches)
- poor concentration
- irritability
- fear of personal harm
- regressive behavior (clinging, whining)
- nightmares
- aggressive behavior at home or school
- bed wetting
- anxiety & fears
- confusion
- eating difficulty
- withdrawal/social isolation
- attention-seeking behavior

Early Adolescence (Ages 11 through 14)
- sleep disturbance
- withdrawal/isolation from peers
- increase or decrease in appetite
- loss of interest in activities
- rebelliousness
- generalized anxiety
- school difficulty, including fighting
- fear of personal harm
- physical ailments (e.g., bowel problems)
- poor school performance
- depression
- concentration difficulties

Adolescence (Ages 14 through 18)
- numbing
- intrusive recollections
- sleep disturbance
- anxiety and feelings of guilt
- eating disturbance
- poor concentration and distractibility
- psychosomatic symptoms (e.g., headaches)
- antisocial behavior (e.g., stealing)
- apathy
- aggressive behavior
- agitation or decrease in energy level
- poor school performance
- depression
- peer problems
- withdrawal
- increased substance abuse
- decreased interest in the opposite sex
- amenorrhea or dysmenorrhea

What types of <u>personal</u> reactions can teachers expect after a crisis situation has occurred?

As in the case of children, the answer to this question is dependent on a number of variables including personal history, personality variables, severity and proximity of the event, level of social support and type and quality of intervention. The fact that some of the possible immediate adult reactions to a crisis are confusion, disorganization and difficulty in decision making, underscores the need for a preplanned, practiced and organized response plan. Longer term reactions that are experienced by adults are:

Adulthood
- denial
- feelings of detachment
- unwanted, intrusive recollections
- depression
- concentration difficulty
- anxiety
- psychosomatic complaints
- hypervigilance
- withdrawal
- eating disturbance
- irritability and low frustration tolerance
- sleep difficulty
- poor work performance
- loss of interest in activities once enjoyed
- emotional and mental fatigue
- emotional lability
- marital discord

Since teachers are likely to be affected by the crisis situation, it is imperative that they receive the appropriate support and intervention. Without such intervention, they will be limited in their ability to meet the needs of their students. It is important that teachers have a forum to discuss their own feelings and reactions to the crisis and receive support. Teachers usually look to other teachers, and possibly school support personnel (e.g., psychologist, social worker, guidance counselor) to share their feelings. Family and friends outside the school environment can also serve as important sources of support. As with their students, most teachers will show a full recovery from the crisis situation. However, if the symptoms outlined above persist and continue to interfere with functioning, professional consultation may be beneficial.

What can classroom teachers do to address the reactions of their students during a crisis situation?

Teachers are on the "front lines" during and following a crisis situation. They have spent the most time with their students and often know them better than anyone in the school. Therefore, teachers are likely to be in a good position to provide early and ongoing intervention. However, they are also in a very difficult position because they need to remain composed and in control for their students at a time when they themselves may be experiencing a flood of emotions in response to the crisis. Classroom teachers can find this especially difficult if they are not trained in crisis response and/or are not familiar with how to address the needs of their students following a crisis. Following are interventions that teachers can provide to address the reactions of their students to a crisis situation:

- After obtaining the facts regarding the crisis, *as well as permission from the principal to disclose them*, classroom teachers should accurately and honestly explain what has happened to their students. Their students should be told the information in a manner that they can understand, taking such variables as age and functioning levels into consideration.

- Teachers can, and most of the time should, consult with school personnel who are trained in crisis response and crisis intervention (e.g., school psychologist, school social worker, guidance counselors) on how to most effectively address their students' reactions to the crisis.

- It is often helpful when teachers model appropriate expression of feelings for their students and let them know that they have permission to verbalize what they are experiencing. It is important that teachers remain in control of their own emotions while dealing with their students, a task that may be difficult given that teachers themselves may have been significantly affected by the crisis. Children tend to look toward adults to assess how to react to a situation. A teacher who is experiencing difficulty may not model the optimal ways of coping and expressing feelings.

- If a teacher is unable to function adequately and meet the immediate needs of his/her students, another school official may need to replace the teacher temporarily or help him/her deal with the students. Every attempt should be made to keep the classroom teacher with his/her students.

- Education of students regarding likely responses to the crisis is essential. Students should not feel they are "abnormal" or that they are "going crazy." Explaining to students that they will likely have a "normal reaction to an abnormal situation" can be helpful for them. Teachers may wish to share the age appropriate reactions described in this document.

- Students need to be warned that they may experience waves of strong emotions and coached on how to effectively deal with them (e.g., by talking to others, looking to others for support).

- The strong emotional reactions to a crisis situation are usually overcome in one to six weeks following the crisis. The long-term effects outlined above, however, could take weeks to months to dissipate.

- Classroom teachers should be vigilant for students who are experiencing significant difficulty in comparison to peers, and who may require additional and more individualized crisis intervention. Criteria for determining which students require additional intervention is outlined below.

- It is imperative that students, as a group, be given the opportunity to discuss their feelings and reactions to the crisis situation. The world as they know it has been threatened, their security undermined. They need to be able to discuss these feelings and know that their fears and reactions are shared by others.

- When students are discussing their feelings, teachers need to listen in a noncritical and non-judgmental manner, with empathy and support. It is important that teachers communicate to the students that they understand the students' feelings and as previously indicated, that their feelings are normal reactions to an abnormal situation. Students who are hesitant to verbalize their feelings should be encouraged to do so but demands to verbalize should be avoided.

- The students should be given the opportunity to express themselves through other modes of communication (e.g., writing, and perhaps drawing for younger children), especially those students who are hesitant to verbalize their feelings.

- Teachers can develop classroom activities and assignments, and homework assignments that address students' feelings regarding the crisis. Assignments that are a catalyst for group discussion are best and may facilitate empowerment at a time when many individuals feel a sense of hopelessness and vulnerability.

- Crisis intervention is ongoing. Therefore, future discussions may need to ensue and address residual feelings regarding the crisis. Some students may not experience a reaction to the crisis until days or weeks later. Teachers need to remain sensitive to this fact and remain vigilant to reactions for some time after the crisis. Some students may even try to convince others that they were not affected, and then suddenly show a strong emotional reaction.

When should teachers refer students for more individualized assessment and intervention?

With support from school personnel and their families, and the passage of time, most students will be able to recover from the effects of a crisis and return to pre-crisis functioning. They will be able to meet the demands of their environment, most particularly the school environment. However, there are those students, due to their own psychological makeup (including history and ability to obtain and respond to support), and the severity and proximity of the precipitating event, who will continue to experience difficulties which interfere with functioning. These students are in need of further, and probably more individualized intervention.

The following are guidelines for determining which students should be referred to counselors for additional intervention:

- students who can not engage adequately in classroom assignments and activities after a sufficient amount of time has passed since the crisis and after a majority of their peers are able to do so,
- students that continue to exhibit high levels of emotional responsiveness (e.g., crying, tearfulness) after a majority of their peers have discontinued to do so,
- students who appear depressed, withdrawn and non-communicative,
- students who continue to exhibit poorer academic performance and decreased concentration,
- students who express suicidal or homicidal ideation, or students who are intentionally hurting themselves (e.g., cutting themselves),
- students who exhibit an apparent increased usage of alcohol or drugs,
- students who gain or lose a significant amount of weight in a short period of time,
- students who exhibit significant behavioral changes, and
- students who discontinue attending to their hygienic needs.

Conclusion

The immediacy and unpredictability of crisis situations often leave individuals with a sense of worry, vulnerability and distrust. A school system is unique in that it brings together individuals of all ages and professionals from numerous disciplines. Effective response to a crisis capitalizes on the resources within the school environment. *A Crisis Response Team that identifies and responds to a crisis in a unified and collaborative manner can alter the aftermath of a crisis.*

D. Parent Guidelines for Crisis Response

Reprinted from *A Practical Guide for Crisis Response in Our Schools*
© 2003 by The American Academy of Experts in Traumatic Stress—Reproduced with Permission
368 Veterans Memorial Highway, Commack New York 11725
Tel. (631) 543-2217 • Fax (631) 543-6977 • www.aaets.org • www.schoolcrisisresponse.com

In an effort to help you to understand and deal effectively with your child's reactions to a crisis situation, our district is providing you with this information. This literature is part of a larger district-wide Crisis Response Plan intended to help our school community deal more effectively with a crisis by providing appropriate support and intervention.

What is a crisis and what is crisis response?

A crisis is a traumatic event that is typically unpredicted and overwhelming for those who experience it. This situation may be volatile in nature and, at times, may involve threat to the survival of an individual or groups of individuals. Moreover, a crisis state may result upon exposure to drastic and tragic change in an individual's environment which has become common and familiar to them. This alteration in the status quo is unwanted, frightening, and often renders a person with a sense of vulnerability and helplessness. Ultimately, with successful intervention, the equilibrium is restored between the environment and the individual's perception of their world as a safe and secure place. Examples of crises that can potentially have a large scale effect on the students, faculty and administrators in a school building or district include: an accident involving a student or faculty member, a suicide or death of a student or faculty member, severe violence (e.g., gang fight), hostage taking, fire at school or a natural disaster (e.g., hurricane).

Crisis response, as it pertains to the school environment, is a proactive, organized and well thought out plan to a crisis situation that has adversely affected many individuals in a school district, including students, faculty and administrators.

Why a Crisis Response Plan?

Research has revealed that schools are increasingly more prone to crisis situations that adversely affect large numbers of students and faculty. The rise in adolescent suicide, increased assaults on teachers, high levels of substance abuse among students and increased violence in the schools are some of the reasons cited. Research has also indicated that today's school districts need to contend with reactions to new types of trauma. For example, hostage taking, sniper attacks, murders, terrorist activities and bomb scares were almost nonexistent in the schools 30 years ago, but today occur with greater frequency.

Thus, it is strongly suggested that school districts need to be prepared for a crisis situation that can potentially affect the functioning of their students, faculty and administrators. Lerner (1997) comments:

"There are two kinds of beach front homeowners on the south shore of Long Island: those who have faced serious erosion, and those who will. Similarly, there are two kinds of schools: those that have faced a serious crisis situation, and those that will."

Research has emerged over the past ten years supporting a proactive approach to a crisis, as opposed to one that is reactive in nature, is much better in dealing effectively with a large scale crisis situation. A reactive approach is spontaneous, and not fully thought out, planned, or practiced, and can result in a response that is less effective in meeting the immediate, and possibly the long-term needs of the students, faculty and administrators.

In summary, a proactive approach to a crisis is one that is organized, planned and practiced and more likely results in a response that can have a dramatic effect on reducing the short and long-term consequences of the crisis on the individuals in a school district.

What types of behaviors/reactions can parents expect from their *child* after a crisis situation has occurred?

The manner in which people react to crisis situations is dependent on a number of variables including personal history, personality variables, severity and proximity of the event, level of social support and the type and quality of intervention. While no two people respond to situations, including crisis situations, in exactly the same manner, the following are often seen as <u>immediate</u> reactions to a significant crisis:

- shock, numbness,
- denial or inability to acknowledge the situation has occurred,
- dissociative behavior—appearing dazed, apathetic, expressing feelings of unreality,
- confusion,
- disorganization,
- difficulty making decisions, and
- suggestibility.

It is important to note that most children will recover from the effects of a crisis with adequate support from family, friends and school personnel. Their response to a crisis can be viewed as "a normal response to an abnormal situation." While the emotional effects of the crisis can be significant and can potentially influence functioning for weeks to months, most children will evidence a full recovery.

Following are descriptions of responses likely to observed in children:

- **Regression in Behavior**: Children who have been exposed to a crisis often exhibit behaviors that are similar to children younger than themselves. This is especially true of toddlers, preschool and elementary school children. They may return to behavior that was abandoned long ago (e.g., thumb sucking, bed-wetting, fears of the dark). Traumatized children may also exhibit separation anxiety, clinging to parents and resistance to leaving the parents' side. They may resist going to bed alone. Bladder and bowel control may be temporarily lost in younger children.

- **Increase in Fears and Anxiety**: Children also exhibit an increase in their fears and worries. They may again become afraid of situations they mastered long ago. As mentioned above they may become fearful of the dark and refuse to go to bed alone. A school phobia may emerge where the child refuses to go to school for fear of something happening and/or fear of leaving his/her parents. They may openly verbalize their fear of the crisis occurring again in the school. It is important that parents do not allow the child to remain home as a means to deal with his/her anxiety. This will result in the anxiety increasing once the child needs to return to school. Due to the increase in fears, additional demands are made for parent attention and support. Adolescents may experience a more generalized anxiety and not the specific types of fears that are seen in younger children.

- **Decreased Academic Performance and Poor Concentration**: Given the increase in anxiety and the disruption a crisis can have on children's sense of safety and security, there is a decrease in the amount of mental energy and focus available to learn and complete academic assignments.

- **Increased Aggression and Oppositional Behavior, and Decreased Frustration Tolerance**: Children who have been exposed to a crisis can experience difficulty controlling their anger and frustration. Situations that would not have caused a heightened emotional response prior to the crisis, can post-crisis result in an aggressive response and/or expression of frustration. Adolescents may also exhibit an increase in oppositional behavior, refusing to live by the rules and regulations of school and home, and/or meet their responsibilities (e.g., chores, academic assignments). Some adolescents may resort to antisocial behavior (e.g., stealing).

- **Increased Irritability, Emotional Liability and Depressive Feelings**: Children can also exhibit stronger and more variable emotional responses to situations. There could be symptoms of depression that include general sense of sadness, difficulty falling and remaining asleep or sleeping more than normal, change in eating habits, loss of interest in activities once enjoyed, social withdrawal, mental and physical fatigue and/or suicidal ideation. In younger children there may be an increase in irritability and moodiness.

- **Denial**: In an effort to cope with the psychological and emotional ramifications of a crisis, certain children and adolescents will deny that a crisis has occurred and/or deny the significance of a crisis. A child whose mother has died suddenly may demand that he can return home so that they can watch their favorite television program together. An adolescent whose favorite teacher was badly injured in a car accident may insist that he will recover fully, despite the medical evidence that indicates that this will not happen. Children who continue to utilize denial to cope may need to be confronted in a sensitive but straight forward manner. Anger and resentment may be expressed when confronting the child with the reality. In time, and with support, children do come to accept the reality of a situation.

What types of reactions may *parents* experience after a crisis situation has occurred that involves themselves and/or their child?

As in the case of children, the answer to this question is dependent on a number of variables including personal history, personality variables, severity and proximity of the event, level of social support and type and quality of intervention. The fact that some of the possible immediate adult reactions to a crisis are confusion, disorganization and difficulty in decision making, underscores the need for a preplanned, practiced and organized response plan. Longer term reactions that are experienced by adults are:

- denial
- feelings of detachment
- unwanted, intrusive recollections
- depression
- concentration difficulty
- anxiety
- psychosomatic complaints
- hypervigilance
- withdrawal
- eating disturbance
- irritability and low frustration tolerance
- sleep difficulty
- poor work performance
- loss of interest in activities once enjoyed
- emotional and mental fatigue
- emotional lability
- marital discord

Since you are likely to be affected by the crisis situation, either directly through exposure to the crisis or indirectly through your child's exposure, it is imperative that you receive the appropriate support and intervention. Without such intervention, you will be limited in your ability to meet the needs of your child. It is important that you have a forum to discuss your own feelings and reactions to the crisis and receive support. You should look to family members, other parents in the district, friends, and/or school support personnel (e.g., psychologist, social worker, guidance counselor) to share your feelings. It is likely that the school will have a meeting for parents to discuss the crisis, and offer them support and education. You are encouraged to attend. As with your child, you will most likely not experience long-term effects because of the crisis. However, if the symptoms outlined above persist and continue to interfere with your ability to function, professional consultation may be beneficial.

What can parents do to address the reactions of their child to a crisis situation?

As parents you are probably the most influential factor in the recovery of your child from the emotional consequences of a crisis. Since you are the most emotionally involved with your child, your support, encouragement and reassurance is of utmost importance in your child's recovery. While you may be frequently frustrated that you can't do more to alleviate your child's suffering, you need to realize that your efforts can not be replaced by anyone else.

As a parent of a child exposed to a crisis, you face several challenges in your effort to help your him/her. First, you may experience guilt because you were unable to protect your child from the wrath of the crisis. Even though this guilt may have no foundation in reality, it is real to you, and needs to be kept under control so that it doesn't disable you from focusing on your child's needs. Second, you need to keep yourself under control in a situation that may have been very emotional and traumatizing to you. This is especially true if you were also exposed to the crisis situation. You need to realize that you can suffer secondary traumatization due to your child's exposure to a crisis. As discussed above, you need to attend to your own emotional responses and seek intervention. While you need to be fully involved in your child's recovery, time for yourself will do more to help your child. Following are interventions that you can provide to address the reactions of your child to a crisis situation.

- Speak to your child regarding the crisis and provide him/her with accurate information regarding the crisis in a language that he/she can understand.
- Your child needs to feel that he/she is allowed to express his/her thoughts and feelings regarding the crisis without the fear that he/she will be judged negatively. It is important for you to listen carefully to your child and show him/her that you understand what he/she is feeling and thinking.
- Your child needs constant reassurance that things will get better and that in the long-term things will improve. This should only be stated if it is indeed true. No false statements regarding the future should be made in an effort to help your child feel better in the present. This will only lead to false hopes and distrust in the future.
- Reassure your child that you will continue to "be there" for him/her, and that you will see them through the aftermath of the crisis.
- Your child may need additional affection in the form of hugs and other physical contact.
- You will most likely need to keep in touch with your child's teacher to monitor his/her academic performance.
- You will need to spend additional individualized time with your child. Try to structure your time with him/her by playing games, having discussions and going places. During your time together, focus a majority of your attention on your child.
- You will need to monitor the adjustment of your adolescent from somewhat of a distance since his/her primary support group may be his/her peers. Don't be hesitant to ask your adolescent child how he/she is coping even though you may expect an answer of "fine." The fact that you ask will most likely be important to your adolescent child, even though he/she may not show this.
- Monitor your adolescent child for increased use of alcohol or drugs. There may be an attempt to "self-medicate" by using these substances. Also monitor your adolescent child for increased symptoms of depression.
- Regardless of your adolescent child's response to you, reassure him/her that you are there if he/she needs help and/or assistance. You may want to outline just how you can help him/her (e.g., by talking, by getting him/her professional help).

When should your child receive additional help in the form professional intervention?

With support and reassurance from you and others in your family, intervention from school personnel, and the passage of time, your child should be able to recover from the effects of a crisis and return to pre-crisis functioning. He/she should be able to meet the demands of his/her environment, most particularly his/her home and school environments. However, there is a chance that your child, due to the nature of the crisis itself and due to his/her psychological makeup, history and ability to respond to support, will continue to experience difficulties which interfere with his/her functioning. If the symptoms outlined above persist, your child is probably in need of further, and probably more individualized, intervention. The following are guidelines for determining if your child requires additional intervention from professionals trained in addressing traumatic stress:

- your child can not engage adequately in home-based responsibilities and in school-based assignments and activities after a sufficient amount of time has passed since the crisis and after a majority of his/her peers are able to do so,
- your child continues to exhibit high levels of emotional responsiveness (e.g., crying, tearfulness) after a majority of his/her peers have discontinued to do so,
- your child appears depressed, withdrawn and non-communicative,
- your child continues to exhibit poorer academic performance and a decreased capacity for concentration,
- your child expresses suicidal or homicidal ideation, or your child is intentionally hurting him/herself (e.g., cutting him/herself),
- your child exhibits an apparent increase usage of alcohol or drugs,
- your child gains or loses a significant amount of weight in a short period of time,
- your child evidences significant changes in behavior, and
- your child discontinues attending to his/her hygienic needs.

What can school personnel provide in the form of support and intervention for your child?

The Crisis Response Plan discussed earlier incorporates support and intervention to help your child return to pre-crisis functioning and cope effectively with the crisis. Teachers have been made aware through similar literature as this, disseminated by the district, on how to address their students' needs. The building psychologist, social worker and/or guidance counselors can consult with teachers to help them deal effectively with their students' reaction to the crisis. Discussions led by support staff and/or the classroom teacher regarding the crisis can be implemented if deemed necessary. These discussions hopefully will afford your child a forum in order to express his/her feelings regarding the crisis and understand how his/her classmates are coping. Specialized work may be assigned that can help your child to deal with the emotional aftermath of the crisis.

The classroom teachers can also assess their students' functioning and recovery from the crisis. They should be sensitive to the effects of the crisis on their students and can adjust the classroom demands accordingly. They can also monitor their students for signs that additional, and more individualized intervention is needed. If your child is experiencing difficulty in class and/or is referred to support staff for assessment and/or intervention, you will be notified as soon as possible.

Conclusion

The immediacy and unpredictability of crisis situations often leave individuals with a sense of worry, vulnerability and distrust. A school system is unique in that it brings together individuals of all ages and professionals from numerous disciplines. Effective response to a crisis capitalizes on the resources within the school environment. *A Crisis Response Team that identifies and responds to a crisis in a unified and collaborative manner can alter the aftermath of a crisis.*

E. Identifying Students "At-Risk" for Violent Behavior: A Checklist of "Early Warning Signs"

Reprinted from *A Practical Guide for Crisis Response in Our Schools*
© 2003 by The American Academy of Experts in Traumatic Stress—Reproduced with Permission
368 Veterans Memorial Highway, Commack New York 11725
Tel. (631) 543-2217 • Fax (631) 543-6977 • www.aaets.org • www.schoolcrisisresponse.com

Violence continues to impact our schools and, in a sense, we should consider all of our students "at-risk." The purpose of this Infosheet is to assist parents and school personnel in identifying children and adolescents who are at *greater risk* for engaging in violent behavior.

The following checklist of "early warning signs" will facilitate identification of students who may be in need of intervention. The greater the number of items that are checked, the greater the potential for violent acting-out behavior. For help, turn to individuals who regularly work with at-risk children and adolescents—professionals in the fields of education, law enforcement, social services, medicine, mental heath, etc.

Children and adolescents at-risk may:
- ❏ express self-destructive or homicidal ideation
- ❏ express feelings of hopelessness
- ❏ have a history of self-destructive behavior
- ❏ give away possessions
- ❏ articulate specific plans to harm self and/or others
- ❏ appear withdrawn
- ❏ engage in "bullying" other children
- ❏ evidence significant changes in mood
- ❏ have difficulty with impulse control
- ❏ experience sleep and eating disturbances
- ❏ evidence significant changes in behavior
- ❏ have experienced prior trauma/tragedy
- ❏ engage in substance abuse
- ❏ have been/are victims of child abuse
- ❏ become involved with gangs
- ❏ have experienced a significant loss
- ❏ have been tormented and/or teased by others
- ❏ evidence a preoccupation with fighting
- ❏ evidence a preoccupation with television
- ❏ have a history of antisocial behavior
- ❏ programs/movies with violent themes
- ❏ evidence a low tolerance for frustration
- ❏ evidence a preoccupation with games with violent themes
- ❏ externalize blame for their difficulties
- ❏ evidence a preoccupation with guns and other weapons
- ❏ have harmed small animals
- ❏ have access to a firearm
- ❏ have engaged in fire setting
- ❏ have brought a weapon to school
- ❏ evidence persistent bed wetting
- ❏ evidence frequent disciplinary problems
- ❏ appear/acknowledge feeling depressed
- ❏ exhibit poor academic performance
- ❏ talk about not being around
- ❏ have been frequently truant from school

F. Preventing Violent Tragedies in Our Schools

Reprinted from *A Practical Guide for Crisis Response in Our Schools*
© 2003 by The American Academy of Experts in Traumatic Stress—Reproduced with Permission
368 Veterans Memorial Highway, Commack New York 11725
Tel. (631) 543-2217 • Fax (631) 543-6977 • www.aaets.org • www.schoolcrisisresponse.com

Today, we are faced with an increase in violence including assaults and gang activity. We are seeing an increase in the frequency of substance abuse, self-mutilation, suicide, abandonment of newborn babies, and serious injuries and deaths from automobile accidents. We are also contending with new types of violence including terrorist attacks, hostage-taking, snipers, murders, "hit lists," threatening graffiti, bomb scares and real bombs.

In response to this disturbing trend, The American Academy of Experts in Traumatic Stress published *A Practical Guide for Crisis Response in Our Schools*. This guide is being utilized as a "Crisis Response Plan" by school districts across the country. The importance of having an organized and preconceived strategy for responding effectively in the wake of a school-based tragedy cannot be underscored enough.

In the face of a rapidly changing zeitgeist, we must address means of *preventing* violent tragedies in our schools. Specifically, we need to assist children in developing their communication, coping and problem-solving skills. The following should be considered.

We must help our children to:

- develop and enhance their communication and problem-solving skills,

- understand the importance of articulating their feelings about themselves and for others,

- know that it is okay to err on the side of caution when expressing their concerns about others,

- regularly remind them that they can turn to school support personnel who will take the time to listen and respond to them,

- identify physiological changes in their bodies which may precede or coincide with feelings of frustration and anger,

- understand which behaviors/actions cause others to become frustrated and angry,

- become aware of and identify negative self-statements that generate feelings of frustration and anger,

- learn to replace self-defeating statements with positive coping statements, and

- learn to make more adaptive goal-directed decisions when faced with feelings of frustration (e.g., deciding to walk-away from altercations... to take a few moments to "cool down"... to express oneself assertively... to implement relaxation techniques, or to utilize conflict resolution skills).

G. Sample Emergency Contact List (For Out-of-School Hours)

Sample

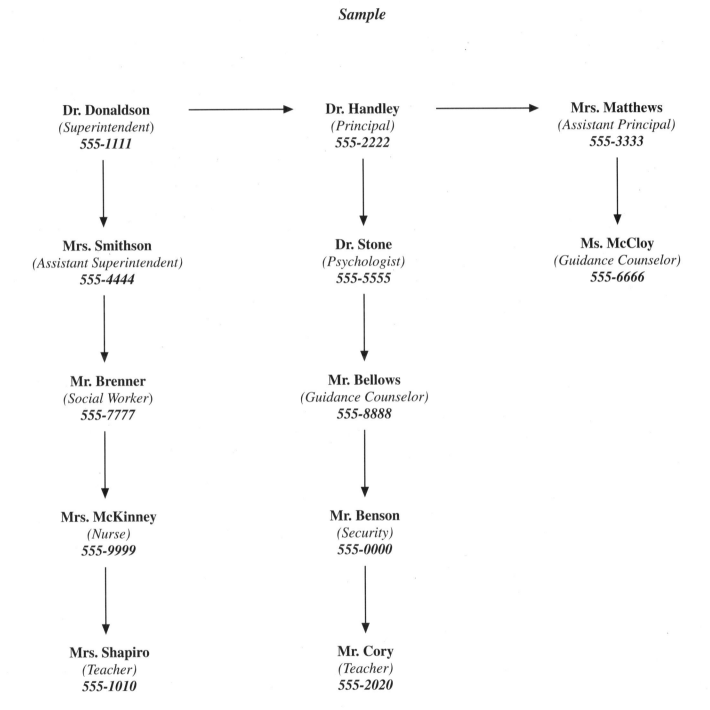

Dr. Donaldson
(Superintendent)
555-1111

Dr. Handley
(Principal)
555-2222

Mrs. Matthews
(Assistant Principal)
555-3333

Mrs. Smithson
(Assistant Superintendent)
555-4444

Dr. Stone
(Psychologist)
555-5555

Ms. McCloy
(Guidance Counselor)
555-6666

Mr. Brenner
(Social Worker)
555-7777

Mr. Bellows
(Guidance Counselor)
555-8888

Mrs. McKinney
(Nurse)
555-9999

Mr. Benson
(Security)
555-0000

Mrs. Shapiro
(Teacher)
555-1010

Mr. Cory
(Teacher)
555-2020

H. Sample Announcement to Students & Faculty

Note: *This sample is fictitious and is provided as an example to be used by the school principal, or his/her designee, to formally address the students and faculty. This announcement will require modifications based upon the nature of the crisis, age of the student population, wishes of the victim's family, etc.*

"You may have noticed that our flag is flying at half-mast. Last night, two of our students were involved in an automobile accident on Oak Ridge Drive. Barry Roth and Steven Kent, who were driving together, both died as a result of their injuries. As more information becomes available, including funeral arrangements, I will speak to you again. This is a terrible tragedy for the Kennedy High School community and our thoughts are with the Roth and Kent families.

We need to be here for each other at this difficult time. Anyone who feels the need to talk should report to our school library, where you can speak with our school psychologists, social workers and guidance counselors. Please sign *out* of your assigned class and *in* at the library. Should you need to speak with someone after school hours, you can contact the Long Island Crisis Center at (516) 679-1111. Their services are confidential and free of charge.

I am requesting that seniors who have driven to school remain on campus for the next few days so that we can all be here to help each other. If you see someone in need, please reach out to support and comfort them—and encourage them to speak with someone in the library."

I. Sample Announcement to the Media

Note: *This sample is fictitious and is provided as an example to be utilized by the school principal, or his/her designee, to address the media. This announcement will require modifications based upon confidentiality issues, wishes of the victim's family, nature of the crisis (e.g., will the crisis draw national attention), etc.*

"My name is Dr. Jonathan Miller and I am the principal of Cedar Creek Middle School. We learned that one our seventh grade students, Melanie Cole, was abducted this morning by two men as she stepped-off of her school bus in front of the school. We subsequently learned that the police found and identified Melanie's body near Cedar Creek just two blocks east of the school. This is a terrible tragedy for Melanie's family, our school and our community. We have been in contact with Melanie's parents and they have requested that we all understand their need for privacy at this difficult time.

Our school implemented our Crisis Response Plan. District psychologists, social workers, guidance counselors, administrators and teachers who are members of our school's Crisis Response Team immediately went into action and are providing help for our students and faculty. Fortunately, our school family is pulling together at this difficult time. Thank you."

J. Sample Memorandum to the Faculty

Note: *This sample is fictitious and is provided as an example to be utilized by the school principal, or his/her designee, in writing to the school faculty. This memorandum will require modifications based upon confidentiality issues, wishes of the victim's family, nature of the crisis, age of student population, funeral arrangements, etc.*

CONFIDENTIAL MEMORANDUM

To: High School Faculty
From: Dr. Mary Beth Johnson, Principal
Date: January 7, 2002

One of our seniors, Lawrence Fogel, died last night from a self-inflicted gunshot to his head. This is a tragedy for the Fogel family, our school and our community. I will be addressing the school this morning over the P.A. I have spoken with Mr. and Mrs. Fogel who have asked that I report the following information to our students and staff:

> "Due to pressures beyond our understanding, Larry took his own life with a gun he supposedly obtained on the streets. He left a note indicating that he thought his life was hopeless.... We have been told that Larry died instantly from the gunshot. A funeral will be held on Thursday, January 10th at 11:00 AM at Pine Hill Memorial Chapel on East Brook Drive."
>
> —Mr. Ben Fogel

Our Crisis Response Team met this morning, before school hours, and is requesting that you direct students who need to speak with someone to the guidance lounge. Our psychologists, social workers and guidance counselors will be available. Students are asked to sign *out* of their assigned class and *in* at the lounge.

It will be important that we make every effort to maintain regular classroom instruction. However, I understand that for many of the students this will be difficult. Please feel free to read the statement from Mr. Fogel if you believe it is appropriate, and use it to facilitate discussion about this tragedy. You may wish to turn to the *Practical Guide for Crisis Response in Our Schools* for suggestions on how to best help the students. Copies have been disseminated in your department offices. Finally, tests scheduled for this Wednesday should be postponed due to funeral arrangements.

I understand that this may be a very difficult time for you and we need to be here for each other. If you feel the need to speak to someone, please contact our school psychologist, Dr. Mark Turner, at Ext. 250. Your contacts with him will remain strictly confidential.

K. Sample Letter to Parents

Note: *This sample is fictitious and is provided as an example to be utilized by the school principal, or his/her designee, in writing to parents. This letter will require modifications based upon confidentiality issues, wishes of the victim's family, nature of the crisis, age of student population, funeral arrangements, etc.*

Dear Parents,

On Tuesday afternoon, one of our 4th grade students, Reinaldo Garcia, was involved in an automobile accident with his mother. Mrs. Garcia is in stable condition in the intensive care unit of Central Hills Community Hospital. Reinaldo died as a result of his injuries. This is a tragedy for the Garcia family, our school and our community.

Reinaldo was a very bright and popular student at Berry Hill Elementary School. Our District Crisis Response Team has provided support for students and staff. Team members went into each of the classrooms and facilitated discussion with the children about this tragedy. For many, this was their first exposure to death. Some children have met individually with district psychologists, social workers and counselors. I have asked that the parents of these children be contacted.

Although classroom instruction will continue as always, I anticipate that the next few days will be particularly difficult for everyone. Please keep in mind that it is not uncommon for children to exhibit fears, poor concentration, nightmares, physical complaints, withdrawal, eating and sleep difficulties, regressive behaviors, crying and irritability.

Over the course of the days to come, please monitor your child and allow him/her to express feelings in a non-judgmental climate. If you wish to speak with someone concerning your child, please contact our school psychologists, Dr. Gary Sommer or Dr. Veronica Keary at (516) 555-1234.

We need to be here for each other at this difficult time.

Sincerely,

Myra S. Reiss, Ed.D.
Principal, Berry Hill Elementary School

L. A Case Example (Fictitious)

Background

On Saturday, December 8, 2001, at approximately 1:30 AM, three students were killed on the Long Island Expressway on their way home from a party. The automobile in which they were driving struck a light pole and immediately became engulfed in fire. The students were seniors at Harperville Senior High School. One of the students was a well-known athlete, one was a class officer, and one, a popular cheerleader.

The Intervention

Sunday evening, the high school principal, Dr. Handley, was notified by the superintendent of the school district. Dr. Handley began exploring the details of the accident. He contacted the police in order to clarify the time, place, and manner in which the students were killed. Additionally, he spoke with the students' parents, and in one case, an aunt. There was discussion concerning what information would be disclosed to the school community. Dr. Handley called Mrs. Matthews, assistant principal. He then began calling the Crisis Response Team using the Emergency Contact List. Thus, Dr. Handley called Dr. Stone, the school psychologist, who called Mr. Tino, the social worker, and so on. It was agreed that the Crisis Response Team would meet at 6:00 AM, one and one half hours before the faculty and students would begin arriving at school on Monday morning.

Rooms for individual and small group counseling sessions were identified. Several signs were prepared in advance for posting in the hallways. The Crisis Response Team determined that given the popularity and high visibility of these students, additional support from all other schools in the district would be needed. Additionally, it was decided by the Crisis Response Team that a brief emergency staff meeting would take place upon the faculty's arrival at the school. It was discovered that one of the students killed in the accident had a younger sister in the elementary school. The psychologist in that building was informed of the situation. She was going to make a contact with this youngster and her teacher.

As expected, the faculty was shaken by the announcement. Several of the teachers began to sob as the principal reported what he knew at that point in time. The social worker, Mr. Tino, announced where the support staff would be located throughout the day for the students and faculty to receive help. Staff were strongly encouraged to seek assistance either by sending a student or using the intercom system if they felt a need for support from a Crisis Response Team member in the classroom. Members of the Crisis Response Team, namely the psychologist and school nurse, announced their availability beyond school hours for colleagues seeking support. Dr. Handley recommended that teachers postpone administration of tests on this day.

When the students arrived, Dr. Handley made an announcement to the school over the public address system. He stated that the death of these three students was a tragedy and that the school community would "miss them very much." He informed the students that support staff would be available all day if they felt a need to talk and where this staff would be located. Dr. Handley discouraged students and staff from speaking with the media and indicated that he would be addressing them. Signs were posted around the building indicating the location of support personnel. Finally, Dr. Handley asked that students who drove to school not leave the building during the school day.

A letter was prepared by the assistant principal to send home to the parents and guardians of the students. The letter stated the school community was currently facing a crisis, the types of reactions to expect from their children, and a recommendation that parents and guardians closely monitor the reactions of their children. A summary of the methods that the school was utilizing was provided as well as crisis line and emergency numbers in the event that their child was having difficulty coping with the tragedy. A memorandum was placed in faculty mailboxes.

Individual crisis intervention was provided by the psychologists. The social workers and guidance counselors were conducting small group counseling sessions. There was a flow of students into and out of the support groups. A list of all students seen in counseling was maintained. Students who were close to the individuals in the accident were closely monitored and in some cases, contact was made with their parents by guidance counselors. Students were only *encouraged* to talk and express themselves; the request for them to talk was *never* demanded. The parents and/or guardians of high risk students were contacted and referrals were provided for further intervention. Dr. Handley provided staff and students with juice and cookies.

In the classroom, teachers began their classes by addressing the loss with their students. Many of the students were visibly upset. Rather than lecturing, some of the teachers decided to conduct "group discussion" at the suggestion of the Crisis Response Team.

Two local news stations arrived at the school looking to interview faculty and students. A security guard advised them to speak directly with the principal, otherwise they would "have to leave school property." One reporter spoke with Dr. Handley.

At the end of the day, after the students and staff left the building, the Crisis Response Team reconvened. They shared their experiences with each other. A follow-up plan for students who seemed at high risk was developed that ensured that the parents/ guardians of these students were called, and/or met with. Recommendations for close monitoring and/or outside counseling were made. Some of the team members elected to walk around the building for the remainder of the week and offer outreach where needed. Two members planned to continue conducting group counseling on a rotating basis. Several staff and faculty members planned to attend the funerals.

A follow-up faculty meeting was scheduled for the next morning. The purpose of this meeting was to give the latest information to the faculty regarding the tragedy, and to get their feedback regarding what had happened and relevant observations of their students. They were again reminded of the availability of support staff for themselves as well as their students. A meeting was held that evening for parents in the community to address their concerns.

It took approximately six weeks for the school community to adjust to the drastic changes that came about so suddenly and unexpectedly. The students established a memorial fund in the names of the deceased and a tree was planted on the side of the school building in memory of the three students.

M. Traumatic Stress: An Overview

Reprinted from *A Practical Guide for Crisis Response in Our Schools*
© 2003 by The American Academy of Experts in Traumatic Stress—Reproduced with Permission
368 Veterans Memorial Highway, Commack New York 11725
Tel. (631) 543-2217 • Fax (631) 543-6977 • www.aaets.org • www.schoolcrisisresponse.com

Traumatic stress encompasses exposure to events or the witnessing of events that are extreme and/or life threatening. Traumatic exposure may be brief in duration (e.g., an automobile accident) or involve prolonged, repeated exposure (e.g., sexual abuse). The former type has been referred to as "Type I" trauma and the latter form, as "Type II" trauma (Terr, 1991). In North America, four out of ten people are exposed to at least one traumatic event in their lifetime (Meichenbaum, 1994). Approximately, 25% to 30% of individuals who witness a traumatic event may develop chronic posttraumatic stress disorder (PTSD) and other forms of mental disorders (e.g., depression) (Yehuda, Resnick, Kahana, & Giller, 1993). Approximately 50% of individuals who develop PTSD continue to suffer from its effects decades later without treatment (Meichenbaum, 1994). Knowledge about traumatic stress- how it develops, how it manifests, and how it affects the lives of those who suffer with it- is the first step in its assessment and, ultimately, its treatment.

History of Traumatic Stress

Traumatic exposure and its aftermath are not new phenomena. Humans have experienced tragedies and disaster throughout history. Evidence for post-traumatic reactions date back as far as the Sixth century B. C.; early documentation typically involved the reactions of soldiers in combat (Holmes, 1985). Beginning in the 17th century, anecdotal evidence of trauma exposure and subsequent responses were more frequently reported. In 1666, Samuel Pepys wrote about individual's responses to the Great Fire of London (Daly, 1983). It had been reported that the author Charles Dickens suffered from numerous traumatic symptoms after witnessing a tragic rail accident outside of London (Trimble, 1981).

Traumatic stress responses have been labeled in numerous ways over the years. Diagnostic terms applied to symptoms have included *Soldier's Heart, Battle Fatigue, War Neurosis, Da Costa's Syndrome, Tunnel Disease, Railway Spine Disorder, Shell Shock, Gross Stress Reaction, Adjustment Reaction of Adult Life, Transient Situational Disturbance, Traumatic Neurosis, Post-Vietnam Syndrome, Rape Trauma Syndrome, Child Abuse Syndrome, and Battered Wife Syndrome* (Everly, 1995). The *Diagnostic and Statistical Manual of Mental Disorders-Third Edition* (DSM-III) first recognized Posttraumatic Stress Disorder (PTSD) as a distinct diagnostic entity in 1980 (APA, 1980). It was categorized as an anxiety disorder because of the presence of persistent anxiety, hypervigilance, exaggerated startle response, and phobic-like avoidance behaviors (Meichenbaum, 1994). This recognition of stress-related reactions was a major step in the development of an empirical literature base investigating traumatic stress. In 1994, The *Diagnostic and Statistical Manual of Mental Disorders-Fourth Edition* (DSM-IV) was published and the current diagnostic criteria reflect the findings of numerous empirical studies and field trials (APA, 1994).

Types of Traumatic Events

Traumatic events are typically unexpected and uncontrollable. They may overwhelm an individual's sense of safety and security and leave a person feeling vulnerable and insecure in their environment. Events that are abrupt, often lasting a few minutes and as long as a few hours can be referred to as short-term or Type I traumatic events (Terr, 1991). Included within this category are natural and accidental disasters as well as deliberately caused human-made disasters. *Natural disasters* include events such as hurricanes, floods, tornadoes, earthquakes, volcanic eruptions, and avalanches. *Accidental disasters* may include motor vehicle accidents (MVA), boat, train, airplane accidents, fires, and explosions. *Deliberately caused human-made disasters* (i.e., intentional human design or IHD) involve bombings, rape, hostage situations, assault and battery, robbery, and industrial accidents.

Sustained and repeated traumatic events (or Type II traumatic events) typically involve chronic, repeated, and ongoing exposure. Examples include *natural and technological disasters* such as chronic illness, nuclear accidents, and toxic spills. Events resulting from *intentional human design* include combat, child sexual abuse, battered syndrome (i.e., spousal abuse), domestic violence, being taken as political prisoner or prisoner of war (POW), and Holocaust victimization. It is important to consider that research indicates that, despite the heterogeneity of traumatic events, individuals who directly or vicariously experience such events show similar profiles of psychopathology including chronic PTSD and commonly observed comorbid disorders such as depression, generalized anxiety disorder, and substance abuse (Solomon, Gerrity, & Muff, 1992).

Current Diagnostic Criteria and Other Considerations

The DSM-IV stipulates that in order for an individual to be diagnosed with posttraumatic stress disorder, he or she must have experienced or witnessed a life-threatening event and reacted with intense fear, helplessness, or horror. The traumatic event is persistently reexperienced (e.g., distressing recollections), there is persistent avoidance of stimuli associated with the trauma, and the victim experiences some form of hyperarousal (e.g., exaggerated startle response). These symptoms persist for more than one month and cause clinically significant impairment in daily functioning. When the disturbance lasts a minimum of two days and as long as four weeks from the traumatic event, Acute Stress Disorder may be a more accurate diagnosis.

It has been suggested that responses to traumatic experience(s) can be divided into at least four categories (for a complete review, see Meichenbaum, 1994). *Emotional* responses include shock, terror, guilt, horror, irritability, anxiety, hostility, and depression. *Cognitive* responses are reflected in significant concentration impairment, confusion, self-blame, intrusive thoughts about the traumatic experience(s) (also referred to as flashbacks), lowered self-efficacy, fears of losing control, and fear of reoccurrence of the trauma. *Biologically-based* responses involve sleep disturbance (i.e., insomnia), nightmares, an exaggerated startle response, and psychosomatic symptoms. *Behavioral* responses include avoidance, social withdrawal, interpersonal stress (decreased intimacy and lowered trust in others), and substance abuse. The process through which the individual has coped prior to the trauma is arrested; consequently, a sense of helplessness is often maintained (Foy, 1992).

Post-traumatic symptoms often co-occur with other psychiatric conditions; this is referred to as comorbidity. For instance, substance abuse (especially, alcoholism), anxiety (e.g., panic disorder), depression, eating disorders, dissociative disorders, and personality disorders may all co-occur with PTSD. With regard to specific populations, Matsakis (1992) reported that between 40% to 60% of women in treatment for bulimia, anorexia, and obesity had described traumatic experiences at some point in their life. Kilpatrick et al. (1989) reported that, among crime victims with PTSD, 41% had sexual dysfunction, 82% had depression, 27% had obsessive-compulsive symptoms, and 18% had phobias. Sipprelle (1992) reported that personality disorders were especially widespread among Vietnam Veterans. Thus, it is important to assess for comorbid disorders when seeing a patient who presents with trauma-induced symptoms.

Assessment of Traumatic Stress

The clinician working with survivors of traumatic stress and posttraumatic stress disorder must consider the multifaceted nature of these disorders. Meichenbaum (1994) recommends a multimodal approach which involves the collection of information from a number of sources, using several different methods over multiple contacts. For a complete review of assessment measures across victim and survivor populations, see Wilson and Keane (1997).

A comprehensive clinical interview is a primary assessment tool in the evaluation of traumatic stress. Careful questioning during an interview allows the survivor to tell his or her account of the event. Individuals need the opportunity to talk about their experience in a safe, non-judgmental setting. Survivors (and oftentimes, their significant others) need to feel understood and supported as they try to make sense of the traumatic event. Questioning also facilitates a working alliance with the person; the "connection" that the person feels with the treating clinician is often associated with continuation of treatment and psychotherapy treatment outcome (Safran & Segal, 1990; Wolfe, 1992). Questioning allows for the gathering of details about the trauma, assessment of current and past levels of functioning, and the development of a treatment plan. Interviews with family members and significant others may provide further insight into the nature of the trauma and presenting symptomatology.

Commonly-used structured interviews include the Clinician Administered PTSD scale (CAPS; Blake et al., 1990) and the Anxiety Disorders Interview Schedule-IV (ADIS-IV; DiNardo, Brown, & Barlow, 1994). A number of paper-and-pencil assessment measures of PTSD have evolved over the past few years as well. Some of the more popular measures include the PTSD subscale of the Minnesota Multiphasic Personality Inventory (MMPI and MMPI-2; Keane, Malloy, & Fairbank, 1984; Schlenger & Kulka, 1987), the Penn Inventory for PTSD (Hammarberg, 1992) and the Trauma Symptom Inventory (Briere, 1995). Some screening instruments for anxiety and depression that are also useful include the Beck Anxiety Inventory (BAI; Beck, 1993) and Beck Depression Inventory- Second Edition (BDI-II; Beck, Steer, & Brown, 1996). One performance-based measure that has been used successfully with combat, rape, and accident disaster patients is the Stroop Color Word Test (McNally, English, & Lipke, 1993). As indicated earlier, assessment for comorbid disorders must be part of the evaluative process.

Treatment of Traumatic Stress

Many techniques have been used to treat survivors after exposure to traumatic events. Presently, no one form of intervention has been shown to be superior for the treatment of traumatic stress and PTSD. Ochberg (1995) divides treatment methods into four categories. *Education* is the first method. This includes educating the survivor (and their families) about trauma and its effects on daily functioning. Cognitive, behavioral, and physical aspects of the stress response are explored with the individual. The clinician and patient may share books and articles relevant to the treatment of the traumatic symptoms (see Matsakis, 1996). This process helps give meaning to the symptoms that he or she experiences and may ultimately facilitate a sense of control or mastery over them.

The second category involves *holistic health*. This includes physical activity, nutrition, spirituality, and humor as they contribute to the healing of the individual. The clinician functions as both a teacher and a coach to his patient, offering support and encouragement as the individual attempts various ways to appropriately heal him or herself.

The third group of treatment techniques includes methods to enhance *social support* and *social integration*. Included within this category are family therapy and group psychotherapy. The former typically helps to improve communication and cohesion between family members. Group treatment allows individuals to reduce feelings of isolation, share difficult feelings and perceptions regarding the trauma, and learn more adaptive coping strategies.

Finally, there are clinical interventions best described as *therapy*. The goal of most forms of therapy is to help the individual work through their grief, extinguish fear responses, and improve the quality of the individual's life. For example, cognitive-behavior therapy typically relies on exposure strategies to reduce intrusive memories, flashbacks, and nightmares related to the traumatic experience. Exposure to fear-producing stimuli and cognitions in a safe and supportive environment, over time, often reduces the impact of these stimuli on the individual's reactivity (Foa & Kozak, 1986). Cognitive restructuring strategies are also utilized to address the meaning and, oftentimes, distortions in thought processes that accompany traumatic exposure (e.g., "Life is awful," "All people are cruel"). Problem-solving training (D'Zurilla, 1986) may help the individual combat indecisiveness and perceptions of helplessness. Other techniques include relaxation training, and guided imagery-based interventions.

Pharmacological treatment of traumatic stress and PTSD indicates that different medications may affect the multi-faceted symptoms of PTSD. For example, Clonidine has been shown to reduce hyperarousal symptoms. Propranolol, Clonazepam, and Alprazolam appear to regulate anxiety and panic symptoms. Fluoxetine may reduce avoidance and explosiveness whereas re-experiencing of traumatic symptoms and depression may be treated with tricyclic antidepressants and selective serotonin reuptake inhibitors. It is important to note that pharmacotherapy as a sole source of intervention is rarely sufficient to provide complete remission of PTSD (Vargas & Davidson, 1993).

As indicated earlier, traumatic stress and particularly, PTSD, are complex and multi-faceted and consequently, a multimodal assessment is recommended. It is suggested that effective treatment will involve a number of the aforementioned techniques. Future research needs to address the outcomes of combining various treatment approaches and maintaining treatment gains over time.

Conclusion

It has been stated that post-traumatic stress may represent "one of the most severe and incapacitating forms of human stress known" (Everly, 1995, p. 7). Fortunately, traumatic stress and its consequences continue to gain recognition and investigation in the helping professions although, clearly, more research needs to be done. For example, motor-vehicle accidents (MVAs) are quite common and often precipitate traumatic stress and PTSD, yet there is a dearth of literature examining their impact as well as the treatment of survivors of motor-vehicle accidents. There is also a need for greater investigation of secondary traumatic stress reactions. This involves the emotional, cognitive, and behavioral consequences for caregivers who work with traumatized people on a regular basis. That is, through their efforts to help a traumatized population, the helpers themselves, become overwhelmed and are traumatized indirectly or secondarily. Moreover, the research examining the effects of traumatic stress in children is in its infancy. This area is especially crucial to study in light of the growing rates of domestic violence in our society.

Recognition of trauma-related stress is the first step in an individual's road to a healthier life. Medical and mental health providers as well as other workers (e.g., emergency care workers) are in an ideal position to offer information, support, and/or the appropriate referrals to victims of traumatic stress. In fact, Lerner and Shelton (2001) have developed **Acute Traumatic Stress Management** (ATSM) as a means to assist individuals *during* a crisis (see www.atsm.org). Unlike other methods for intervention which are typically employed in the aftermath of a traumatic event such as "demobilizing," "defusing" and "debriefing," ATSM can be used when a person is most suggestible and vulnerable to traumatic stress—while the incident is occurring. ATSM, with its emphasis on offering support within the context of a *facilitative or helping attitudinal climate*, has the potential to stimulate healthy, adaptive functioning. It offers a cognitive "road map" to keep people functioning during traumatic events and ultimately, to mitigate long-term emotional suffering. If more ongoing psychological treatment is indicated, then intervention with a clinician knowledgeable and experienced in working with anxiety and trauma-related difficulties can be a crucial factor in helping victims learn to cope and live life more fully.

Article References

American Psychiatric Association (1980). Diagnostic and statistical manual of mental disorders (3rd ed.). Washington, DC: Author.

American Psychiatric Association (1994). Diagnostic and statistical manual of mental disorders (4th ed.). Washington, DC: Author.

Beck, A.T., Steer, R.A., & Brown, G.K. (1996). Beck Depression Inventory (2nd ed.). San Antonio, TX: The Psychological Corporation.

Beck, A. T. (1993). Beck Anxiety Inventory. San Antonio, TX: The Psychological Corporation.

Blake, D., Weathers, F., Nagy, L., Kaloupek, D., Klauminzer, G., Charney, D., & Keane, T. (1990). Clinician Administered PTSD Scale (CAPS). Boston: National Center for Post-Traumatic Stress Disorder, Behavioral Science Division, Boston VA.

Briere, J. (1995). Trauma Symptom Inventory professional manual. Odessa, FL: Psychological Assessment Resources.

Cummings, N., & Vanden Bos, G.R. (1981). The twenty year Kaiser-Permanente experience with psychotherapy and medical utilization. Health Policy Quarterly, 1, 159-175.

Daly, R.J. (1983). Samuel Pepys and posttraumatic stress disorder. British Journal of Psychiatry, 143, 64-68.

DiNardo, P.A., Brown, T.A., & Barlow, D.H. (1994). Anxiety Disorders Interview Schedule for DSM-IV: Clinician's Manual. New York: Graywind.

D'Zurilla, T.J. (1986). Problem solving therapy: A social competence approach to clinical intervention. New York: Springer.

Everly, G.S. (1995). Psychotraumatology. In G.S. Everly & J.M. Lating (Eds.), Psychotraumatology: Key papers and core concepts in post-traumatic stress (pp. 9-26). New York: Plenum.

Foa, E.B., & Kozak, M.J. (1986). Emotional processing of fear: Exposure to corrective information. Psychological Bulletin, 99, 20-35.

Foy, D.W. (1992). Introduction and description of the disorder. In D. W. Foy (Ed.), Treating PTSD: Cognitive-Behavioral strategies (pp 1-12). New York: Guilford.

Hammarberg, M. (1992). Penn Inventory for posttraumatic stress disorder: Psychometric properties. Psychological Assessment, 4, 67-76.

Holmes, R. (1985). Acts of war. New York: Free Press.

Keane, T.M., Malloy, P.F., & Fairbank, J.A. (1984). Empirical development of an MMPI subscale for the assessment of combat-related post-traumatic stress disorder. Journal of Consulting and Clinical Psychology, 52, 888-891.

Kilpatrick, D. G., Saunders, B.E., Amick-McMullen, A., Best, C.L., Veronen, L.J., & Resnick, H.S. (1989). Victim and crime factors associated with the development of crime-related posttraumatic stress disorder. Behavior Therapy, 20, 199-214.

Lerner, M., & Shelton, R. (2001). Acute Traumatic Stress Management: Addressing emergent psychological needs during traumatic events. New York: The American Academy of Experts in Traumatic Stress.

Matsakis, A. (1992). I can't get over it: A handbook for trauma survivors. Oakland, CA: New Harbinger Publications.

Matsakis, A. (1996). I can't get over it: A handbook for trauma survivors. (2nd ed.) Oakland, CA: New Harbinger Publications.

McNally, R.J., English, G.E., Lipke, H.J. (1993). Assessment of intrusive cognition in PTSD: Use of the modified Stroop paradigm. Journal of Traumatic Stress, 6, 33-42.

Meichenbaum, D. (1994). A clinical handbook/practical therapist manual for assessing and treating adults with post-traumatic stress disorder. Ontario, Canada: Institute Press.

Ochberg, F.M. (1995). Post-traumatic therapy. In G.S. Everly & J.M. Lating (Eds.), Psychotraumatology: Key papers and core concepts in post-traumatic stress (pp. 245-264). New York: Plenum.

Safran, J.D., & Segal, Z.V. (1990). Interpersonal process in cognitive therapy. New York: Basic Books.

Schlenger, W.E., & Kulka, R.A. (1987). Performance of the Keane-Fairbank MMPI scale and other self-report measures in identifying post-traumatic stress disorder. Paper presented at the 95th annual meeting of the American Psychological Association, New York.

Sipprelle, R.C. (1992). A vet center experience: Multievent trauma, delayed treatment type. In D.W. Foy (Ed.), Treating PTSD: Cognitive-Behavioral strategies (pp 13-38). New York: Guilford.

Solomon, S., Gerrity, E.T., & Muff, A.M. (1992). Efficacy of treatments for posttraumatic stress disorder: An empirical review. Journal of the American Medical Association, 268, 633-638.

Terr, L. (1991). Childhood trauma: An outline and overview. American Journal of Psychiatry, 148, 10-20.

Trimble, M.R. (1981). Post-traumatic neurosis. Chicester: Wiley.

Vargas, M.A., & Davidson, J. (1993). Post-traumatic stress disorder. Psychopharmacology, 16, 737-748.

Wilson, J. P., & Keane, T.M. (Eds.). (1997). Assessing Psychological Trauma and PTSD. New York: Guilford.

Wolfe, B.E. (1992). Integrative psychotherapy of the anxiety disorders. In J.C. Norcross & M.R. Goldfried (Eds.), Handbook of Psychotherapy Integration. (pp 373-401). New York: Basic Books.

Yehuda, R., Resnick, H., Kahana, J., & Giller, E. (1993). Long-lasting hormonal alterations to extreme stress in humans: Normative or maladaptive? Psychosomatic Medicine, 55, 287-297.

N. An Overview of Project SAVE

Safe Schools Against Violence in Education
The New York State Guidance Document for School Safety Plans

Reprinted from *A Practical Guide for Crisis Response in Our Schools*
© 2003 by The American Academy of Experts in Traumatic Stress—Reproduced with Permission
368 Veterans Memorial Highway, Commack New York 11725
Tel. (631) 543-2217 • Fax (631) 543-6977 • www.aaets.org • www.schoolcrisisresponse.com

Introduction

Highly publicized tragedies in our schools have had a significant impact on the manner in which educators and communities respond to crises and disaster. Although school violence, especially among adolescents, has shown decreasing trends over the last few years, such evidence has been obscured by recent school shootings and threats of violence. Such events have brought considerable amounts of media attention. However, because of media exposure to such events, there has also been an increasing recognition of the role that school districts play in their response to violence, traumatic events and disaster. Such events include, but are certainly not limited to, acts of threats or intimidation, fighting, assaults, bullying, carrying of weapons and disruptive behavior. Through primary prevention strategies such as education of communities, staff and students about violence and crisis management, there appears to be a growing trend toward making schools safer environments and more conducive to education.

In April of 2001, the New York State Education Department published a document entitled *Project SAVE [Safe Schools Against Violence in Education]: Guidance Document for School Safety Plans*. This handbook was developed collaboratively between the New York State Education Department, New York State Division of Criminal Justice Services, the New York State Police and related state agencies. The *Project SAVE* document compliments a law entitled the *Safe Schools Against Violence in Education Act* (SAVE) which addresses issues of school safety and violence prevention. This was passed by the New York State Legislature and made a law by Governor George E. Pataki on July 24, 2000. *Project SAVE* was developed by New York State for those involved in the educational process from the elementary through secondary levels, across all communities. This legislation made it law for school districts to develop and/or maintain a school safety plan at the district and building levels. Although no one safety management plan will address all needs of all individuals in all school districts, the information provided may serve as a foundation and useful model for other school systems.

The Need for School Safety/Crisis Plans

Efficient crisis plans start with an assessment of the needs of those who will need service. This is where data collected by the Center for Disease Control and Prevention (CDCP) has been most useful. The 1999 Youth Risk Behavior Survey (YRBS) which is conducted by the CDCP and is cited in the New York State *Project SAVE* plan, represents the responses of students in New York State high schools. Among the findings is that approximately 18% of all students and specifically, 27% of male students, report that they have carried a weapon including a gun, knife or club, one or more times within 30 days prior to the survey. Eight percent of students indicated that they have carried a weapon on school property. Moreover, 9% of students said that they were threatened or injured with a weapon on school property within the prior year. Almost 8% of all students reported that they avoided going to school one or more times within 30 days prior to the survey because they felt "unsafe" on their way to or from school and within their school. Within New York, over 500 threats including bomb, arson and anthrax threats, were reported during the 1999-2000 school year.

Setting up the Plan

The State of New York makes it very clear that a pro-active approach to school safety is a priority. It is recommended that there are District-wide School Safety Plans and Building-level Emergency Response Plans developed. Members for the teams should include, but are not limited to, representatives of the School Board, student, teacher, administrator, parent organization member, school safety personnel, other school personnel, community members, local law enforcement officials, local ambulance or other emergency response agencies and any other members the District deems appropriate.

Citing the New York State Center for School Safety (NYSCSS), an outline is recommended to guide schools as they develop and refine their safety plan. The components include:

- **Data Collection** - Assess the information the school already maintains regarding school safety.
- **Data Analysis** - How does the school use this information to identify and prioritize its needs?
- **Problem-Solving** - Attempt to identify what needs to be done.
- **Implementation** - Assess strategies available that could be useful to the school community.
- **Evaluation** - Assess whether or not strategies have been useful.

Some guiding principles are also indicated by the *Project SAVE* and include the following:

- Schools should use existing plans as a foundation for developing a new safety plan.
- Plans should be developed with input from a variety of sources including students, parents, teachers, school leaders, public safety agencies and other key partners.
- Planning should be "comprehensive" and include information ranging from early or primary prevention through crisis response and follow-up.
- Plans should be clear, precise and understandable.
- Plans should define roles and responsibilities of those involved in safety/crisis management while minimizing ambiguity.
- Coordination between public and nonpublic schools should occur as well as recognition of the needs of special school populations, students and staff with disabilities, and limited English-speaking students.
- Plans should be regularly reviewed and updated.

An Example Outline for School Safety Plan

The underlying rationale behind *Project SAVE* is that pro-active, pre-planned responses are more expeditious and useful than "after-the-fact," reactive plans when school districts respond to emergencies and violent incidents. *Project SAVE* suggests the following components for a school safety plan and emphasizes the need for district-specific refinement.

I. Risk Reduction/Prevention and Intervention

As part of a comprehensive safety plan, *Project SAVE* suggests:

- development of crisis/violence prevention/intervention strategies specific to the district.
- addressing communication among students and between students and staff.
- assessing the manner in which potentially violent events are reported.
- establishing conflict resolution training programs, peer mediation programs, youth-run programs, forums for students and school community regarding bullying or violence, and establishes anonymous reporting methods for school violence.
- providing training, drills, and exercises to test components of the emergency response plan.
- providing a description of policies and procedures related to school building security including security guards, hall monitors, visitor/staff badges, sign-in procedure, video surveillance, metal detectors, search dog, and random search.
- describing how the district maintains vital information on each school building, floor plans, school population, number of staff, transportation needs, and phone numbers and other contact information for key school officials.
- providing a policy for primary prevention techniques including how to detect potentially violent or self-destructive behavior for staff, administrators, students, and families.
- identifying sites of potential hazard or emergency including school buildings, playgrounds, athletic fields, off-site field trips and others.

II. Response

In an effort to respond efficiently to an emergency, *Project SAVE* suggests:

- describing policies and procedures for contacting appropriate law enforcement officials in the event of a violent incident.

- developing a system to inform all educational agencies of a disaster or crisis situation including telephone, fax, e-mail, intercom, district radio system and others as appropriate.

- describing the policies and procedures to contact parents, guardians or persons in parental relation to students in the event of early dismissal or violent event.

- describing the district's multi-hazard response plans for responding to threats of violence, intruder, explosive/bomb threat, hostage/kidnaping, hazardous material, natural/weather-related, school bus accident, gas leak, civil disturbance, biological, radiological, epidemic or other critical incidents.

- with regard to *Acts of Violence including Implied or Direct Threat*, districts should use staff trained in de-escalation or other strategies to diffuse the situation, inform Building Principal of implied or direct threat, determine the level of threat (with Superintendent), contact appropriate law enforcement agency (if necessary), isolate the immediate area and evacuate (if necessary), initiate look-down procedure (if necessary), assess need for early dismissal, sheltering or evacuation procedures, and monitor the situation. The building/district should determine the need for the school-based Crisis/Emergency Response Team.

- identification of protocols for appropriate response to emergencies and include determining decision makers, plans to safeguard students and staff, transportation procedures, procedures to notify parents and media and debriefing procedures.

III. Recovery or Postvention

In order to effectively move past a violent or emergency event and restore the district to pre-crisis functioning, *Project SAVE* suggests:

- describing how school district will support Emergency Response Teams or post-incident response teams after the event in the affected school.

- coordinating follow-up and intervention with local community mental health resources.

- processing the response and recovery and re-evaluating current violence prevention and school safety protocols to determine how to refine or improve it.

Conclusion

Although, statistically, school violence and tragedy appears to have declined, the need for a comprehensive school safety plan for school districts nationwide has become paramount. New York State, through *Project SAVE*, mandates a plan for school districts throughout the state at all levels. This safety plan attempts to pre-empt a crisis through primary prevention strategies, develop a plan for when a crisis occurs, and assist a district in its recovery from a crisis situation. As indicated earlier, although no one safety management plan can address all of the needs of all individuals in all school districts, the information provided here may serve as a foundation and useful model for other school systems.

Bibliography

Project SAVE- Safe Schools Against Violence in Education: Guidance document for school safety plans. (April, 2001). New York State Education Department, Albany, NY.

The School Shooter: A threat assessment perspective. (1999). Critical Incident Response Group, National Center for the Analysis of Violent Crime, FBI Academy, Quantico, Virginia.

REFERENCES

Acklin, M.W. (1998). Divorce your spouse, not the kids. http://www.divorcesource.com.

American Academy of Pediatrics (1994). Divorce and children. Elk Grove Village, IL: American Academy of Pediatrics

American Academy of Pediatrics (2000). Suicide and suicide attempts in adolescents. Pediatrics, 105 (4), 871-874.

American Foundation for Suicide Prevention (1998). Youth Suicide. http://www.afsp.org.

American Psychiatric Association (1994). Diagnostic and statistical manual of mental disorders (4th ed.) Washington, DC: Author.

American Psychological Association (1999). Warning signs. http://helping.apa.org.

Anderson, K. (1998). Drug abuse. Probe Ministries, http://www.leaderu.com.

Baker, J.E., Sedney, M., & Gross, E. (1992). Psychological tasks for bereaved children. American Journal of Orthopsychiatry, 62, 105-116.

Baker, J.E., & Sedney, M. (1996). How bereaved children cope with loss: An overview. In C.A. Corr & D.M. Corr (Eds.), Handbook of childhood death and bereavement (pp. 109-129). New York: Springer.

Baum, A., Fleming, R., & Davidson, L.M. (1983). Natural disaster and technological catastrophe. Environment and Behavior, 15, 333-354.

Blanchard, E.B., & Hickling, E.J. (1997). After the crash: Assessment and treatment of motor vehicle accident survivors. Washington, DC: American Psychological Association.

Bowlby, J. (1980). Attachment and loss, Vol. 3 - Sadness and depression. New York: Basic Books.

Center for Disease Control and Prevention (1994). CDC, adolescent and HIV/AIDS. Health Information: Adolescents & HIV/AIDS. CDC National AIDS Clearinghouse.

Center for the Prevention of Sexual and Domestic Violence (2002). What every congregation needs to know about domestic violence: Information for clergy, members of congregations, battered women's programs and human service providers. Center for the Prevention of Sexual and Domestic Violence: Seattle, Washington.

Child Welfare Partnership (1995). Domestic violence summary: The intersection of child abuse and domestic violence. Published by Portland State University.

Critical Incident Response Group (1999). The School Shooter: A threat assessment perspective. National Center for the Analysis of Violent Crime, FBI Academy, Quantico, Virginia.

Davidson, L.E. (1989). Suicide cluster and youth. In C.R. Pfeffer (Ed.), Suicide among youth (pp. 83-99). Washington, DC: American Psychiatric Press.

Dutton, M.A. (1992). Women's response to battering: Assessment and intervention. New York: Springer.

Dutton, M.A. (1994). Post-traumatic therapy with domestic violence survivors. In M.B. Williams & J.F. Sommer (Eds.), Handbook of post-traumatic therapy (pp. 146-161). Westport, CT: Greenwood Press.

Figley, C.R. (1995). Compassion fatigue: Coping with secondary traumatic stress disorder in those who treat the traumatized. New York: Brunner/Mazel.

Forman, S.G. (1993). Coping skills interventions for children and adolescents. San Francisco, CA: Jossey-Bass.

Foy, D.W. (1992). Introduction and description of the disorder. In D. W. Foy (Ed.), Treating PTSD: Cognitive-Behavioral strategies (pp 1-12). New York: Guilford.

Fremouw, W.J., de Perczel, M., & Ellis, T.E. (1990). Suicide risk: Assessment and response guidelines. New York: Pergamon.

Ganley, A. (1989). Integrating feminist and social learning analyses of aggression: Creating multiple models for intervention with men who battered. In P. Caesar & L. Hamberger (Eds.), Treating men who batter (pp. 196-235). New York: Springer.

Gonet, M. (1994). Counseling the adolescent substance abuser: School-based intervention and prevention. Thousand Oaks, CA: Sage.

Graham-Bermann, S. (1994). Preventing domestic violence. University of Michigan research information index. UM-Research-WEB@umich.edu.

Greenstone, J.L., & Levittown, S.C. (1993). Elements of crisis intervention: Crises & how to respond to them. California: Brooks/Cole.

Harmon, M. (1993). Reducing the risk of drug involvement among early adolescents: An evaluation of drug abuse resistance education (DARE), Institute of Criminal Justice and Criminology, University of Maryland.

Hill, D.C., & Foster, Y.M. (1996). Postvention with early and middle adolescents. In C.A. Corr & D.E. Balk (Eds.), Handbook of adolescent death and bereavement (pp. 250-272). New York: Springer.

Klingman, A. (1987). A school-based emergency crisis intervention in a mass school disaster. Professional Psychology: Research and Practice, 18, 604-612.

Kovacs, M., & Beck, A.T. (1977). An empirical approach toward a definition of childhood depression. In J. G. Shchulterbrandt & A. Raskin (Eds.), Depression in childhood: Diagnosis, treatment and conceptual models (pp. 43-57). New York: Raven Press.

Kovacs, M., Goldston, D., & Gatsonis, C. (1993). Suicidal behavior and childhood-onset depressive disorders: A longitudinal investigation. Journal of the American Academy of Child and Adolescent Psychiatry, 32, 8-20.

Kubler-Ross, E. (1969). On death and dying, New York: MacMillan.

Lerner, M. (1988). Perceptions of Desirable Characteristics of Psychotherapists. Doctoral Dissertation. Hofstra University.

Lerner, M. (1997). Early Intervention—A Multidisciplinary Effort. Trauma Response. The American Academy of Experts in Traumatic Stress, Winter, 1997.

Lerner, M. (1998). From the President's Desk. Trauma Response. The American Academy of Experts in Traumatic Stress.

Lerner, M., & Shelton, R. (2001). Acute Traumatic Stress Management: Addressing emergent psychological needs during traumatic events. New York: The American Academy of Experts in Traumatic Stress.

Lockyer, B., & Eastin, D. (1999). Crisis Response Box: Partnering for safe schools. Crime and Violence Prevention Center, Office of the Attorney General, Sacramento, CA.

Matsakis, A. (1996). I can't get over it: A handbook for trauma survivors (2nd ed.). Oakland, CA: New Harbinger Publications.

McKay, M. (1994). The link between domestic violence and child abuse: Assessment and treatment considerations. Child Welfare League of America, 73, 29-39.

McKee, P.W., Jones, R.W., & Richardson, J.A. (1991, November). Student suicide: Educational, psychological issues, and legal issues for schools. Paper presented at the LRP Publications Conference, San Francisco, CA.

Meichenbaum, D. (1994). A clinical handbook/practical therapist manual for assessing and treating adults with post-traumatic stress disorder. Ontario, Canada: Institute Press.

Meyers, A.W., & Craighead, W.D. (1984) (Eds.). Cognitive behavior therapy with children. New York: Plenum Press.

Milkovich, M. (2001). Managing Bomb Threats for School Administrators, Trauma Response (Fall/Winter 2001). The American Academy of Experts in Traumatic Stress.

Missouri Department of Elementary and Secondary Education (1999). State of Missouri School Crisis Response Plan: A workbook and planning guide for school and community leaders. (September, 1999). Department of Elementary and Secondary Education, Missouri.

Morbidity and Mortality Weekly Report (2002). Youth risk behavior surveillance. Surveillance Summaries, MMWR, 51, No. SS-4.

National Association of School Psychologists (1999). Crisis and Loss: Information for educators, Communique, (Special Edition, Spring, 1999).

National Center for Health Statistics (2000). Suicide rates. Division of Data Services, National Center for Health Statistics, Hyattsville, MD.

National Child Abuse and Neglect Data System (2002). NCANDS summary of key findings from calendar year 2000, The Administration of Children and Families, U.S. Department of Health and Human Services.

National Education Association (2001). Crisis Communications Guide & Toolkit, National Education Association, Washington, D.C.

National Highway Traffic Safety Administration (2000). Traffic safety facts 2000. U.S. Department of Transportation, National Center for Statistics & Analysis.

National Household Survey on Drug Abuse (2001). Substance dependence, abuse, and treatment. Substance Abuse and Mental Health Services Administration, U.S. Department of Health and Human Services.

National Institutes of Health (2002). HIV infection in adolescents. Office of Communications and Public Liaison, National Institute of Allergy and Infectious Diseases, National Institutes of Health, Bethesda, MD.

National Institute of Mental Health (1992). Suicide facts. Mental Health Fax4U.

National Resource Center for Safe Schools (2000). Effective Threat Management. National Resource Center for Safe Schools, Portland, OR.

New York State Education Department (2001). Project SAVE - Safe Schools Against Violence in Education: Guidance document for school safety plans. New York State Education Department, Albany, NY.

Noppe, L.D., & Noppe, I.C., (1996). Ambiguity in adolescent understandings of death. In C.A. Corr & D.E. Balk (Eds.), Handbook of adolescent death and bereavement (pp. 25-41). New York: Springer.

Oltjenbruns, K.A. (1996). Death of a friend during adolescence: Issues and impacts. In C.A. Corr & D.E. Balk (Eds.), Handbook of adolescent death and bereavement (pp. 196-215). New York: Springer.

Olweus, D. (1984). Development of stable aggressive reaction: Patterns on males. In R.J. Blanchard & D.C. Blanchard (Eds.), Advances in the study of aggression (pp. 103-137). New York: Academic Press.

Oregon School Boards Association (2001). Never Say Never: Violence and tragedy can strike anywhere. National School Public Relations Association, Salem, OR.

Petersen, S. & Straub, R.L. (1992). School crisis survival guide. West Nyack, NY: The Center for Applied Research in Education.

Pitcher, G.D. & Poland, S. (1992). Crisis intervention in the schools. New York: The Guilford Press.

Planned Parenthood (1998). Fact sheets: Reducing teenage pregnancy. http://www.plannedparenthood.org.

Princeton Survey Research Associates (1996). The 1996 Kaiser family foundation survey on teens and sex: What they say teens today need to know and who they listen to. Menlo Park, CA: The Henry J. Kaiser Family Foundation.

Range, L. (1996). Suicide and life-threatening behavior in childhood. In C.A. Corr & D.E. Balk (Eds.), Handbook of adolescent death and bereavement (pp. 71-88). New York: Springer.

Regier, D.A., & Cowdry, R.W. (1995). Research on violence and traumatic stress (program announcement, PA 95-068). National Institute of Mental Health.

Reynolds, W. (1987). Suicide ideation questionnaire. Odessa, FL: Psychological Assessment Resources.

Reynolds, W. (2002). Reynolds Adolescent Depression Scale -2nd Ed. Psychological Assessment Resources, Inc: Lutz, FL.

Sandoval, J., & Brock, S.E. (1996). The school psychologist's role in suicide prevention. School Psychology Quarterly, 11, 169-185.

Sexual Assault Survivor Services (1996). Facts about domestic violence. http://www.portup.com.

Sexuality Information and Education Council of the United States (2001). Issues and answers: Fact sheet on sexuality education. SIECUS Report, 29(6).

Solomon, S., Gerrity, E.T., & Muff, A.M. (1992). Efficacy of treatments for Posttraumatic Stress Disorder: An empirical review. Journal of the American Medical Association, 268, 633-638.

Straus, M.A., & Gelles, R.J. (1990). Physical violence in American families. New Brunswick, NJ: Transaction Publishers.

Substance Abuse and Mental Health Services Administration (1994). National household survey on drug abuse: Population estimates, 1993. Rockville, MD: Department of Health and Human Services, Substance Abuse and Mental Health Services Administration (DHHS Publication no. (SMA) 94-3017).

Terr, L. (1991). Childhood trauma: An outline and overview. American Journal of Psychiatry, 148, 10-20.

The Center for the Study and Prevention of Violence (1999). http://www.colorado.edu/cspv.

The Henry J. Kaiser Family Foundation (2000). Teen sexual activity: Fact sheet. The Henry J. Kaiser Family Foundation, August 2000.

The Southern Poverty Law Center (1999). Responding to Hate at School: A guide for teachers, counselors and administrators. The Southern Poverty Law Center. Teaching Tolerance, Montgomery, Alabama.

Trump, K. S. (Ed.). (1999). Stopping School Violence: An essential guide. Aspen Publishers, MD.United States Department of Health and Human Services (2002). Preventing teenage pregnancy. HHS Fact Sheet, United States Department of Health and Human Services, Washington, DC: 2002.

United States Department of Justice (2001). Indicators of school crime and safety: 2001. U.S. Departments of Education and Justice, NCES 2002-113/NCJ-190075. Washington, DC: 2001.

Ursano, R.J., McCaughey, B.GF., & Fullerton, C.S. (1994). Individual and community responses to trauma and disaster: The structure of human chaos. New York: Cambridge.

Weaver, J.D. (1995). Disasters: Mental health interventions. Sarasota, FL: Professional Resource Press.

Weinberg, R.B. (1990). Serving large numbers of adolescent victim-survivors: Group interventions at school. Professional Psychology: Research and Practice, 21, 271-278.

Yehuda, R., Resnick, H., Kahana, J., & Giller, E. (1993). Long-lasting hormonal alterations to extreme stress in humans: Normative or maladaptive? Psychosomatic Medicine, 5, 287-297.

The American Academy of Experts in Traumatic Stress®

Administrative Offices, 368 Veterans Memorial Highway, Commack, New York 11725
Telephone (631) 543-2217 • Fax (631) 543-6977 • www.schoolcrisisresponse.com • www.traumatic-stress.org • www.atsm.org

APPLICATION & EXAMINATION FOR
BOARD CERTIFICATION IN SCHOOL CRISIS RESPONSE™

This application will be treated as confidential by The American Academy of Experts in Traumatic Stress, Inc. However, applicants who meet the criteria for Board Certification, and pass the examination, will be identified in *The International Registry of the American Academy of Experts in Traumatic Stress* ™, the association's official directory and referral network. The registry is available in bound copy and can also be accessed directly on the Internet at **www.aaets.org.**

If an applicant is unsuccessful in meeting the criteria for **Board Certification in School Crisis Response (CSCR)** or passing the examination, the applicant will be informed as to the reason for denial. The applicant will be given a second opportunity to provide additional supportive documentation, if needed, and/or a second opportunity to take the examination (revised version). This application reevaluation and/or reexamination will be offered at no additional charge. Moreover, if an applicant is unsuccessful with the second opportunity, the Academy will refund the full fee required for the application/examination process.

In order for The American Academy of Experts in Traumatic Stress to consider you for Board Certification, you must be a Member of the Academy in good standing and:

❏ complete this application in its entirety,
❏ complete the Examination for **Board Certification in School Crisis Response (CSCR),**
❏ sign the declaration, and
❏ enclose one time payment of **$225** for review of your application and examination.
**Please note that your first year Membership dues payment with the Academy will
be waived and you will be entered as a Member of The American Academy of Experts in Traumatic Stress.**

Enclosed is my check for $_____ or please charge $_____ to my ❏ VISA ❏ American Express ❏ MasterCard ❏ Discover Card

_____   _____   _____   _____
Account No.   Expiration Date   Signature   Date

I. INFORMATION

PLEASE PRINT

_____   _____   _____   _____
Last Name   First Name   M.I.   Title (Dr., Mr., Mrs., Ms.)

_____   _____   _____   _____
Street Address   City   State   Zip Code

_____   _____   _____
Home Telephone   Office Telephone(s)   Fax Number

_____   _____   _____
E-mail Address   Highest Educational Degree   Years of Experience in Field

Position (e.g., School Principal, Psychologist, Teacher, etc.):_____

Area(s) of Interest/Specialization:

_____

_____

FOR OFFICE USE ONLY: REVIEWER ID. ____ ____ ____   STATUS CODE: ____ ____

PLEASE PHOTOCOPY THIS APPLICATION & EXAMINATION
AND FAX OR MAIL TO THE ACADEMY'S ADMINISTRATIVE OFFICES FOR PROCESSING

	YES	NO
Have your ever been convicted of a felony?	☐	☐
Have you ever been disciplined for any type of unethical or illegal conduct?	☐	☐
Has your professional license/certification ever been revoked, suspended or limited?	☐	☐
Is there action pending to revoke, suspend, or limit your professional license/certification?	☐	☐
Is there any action pending related to your professional practice?	☐	☐
Have you ever voluntarily surrendered your license/certification?	☐	☐
Do you abuse alcohol or other substances?	☐	☐
Have you ever been denied professional liability insurance or has your insurance ever been canceled or denied renewal?	☐	☐

II. EXAMINATION

Carefully place an **X** over your choices from the examination following this page.

1.	a	b	c	d	e	11.	a	b	c	d	e	21.	a	b	c	d	e	31.	a b c d e
2.	a	b	c	d	e	12.	a	b	c	d	e	22.	a	b	c	d	e	32.	a b c d e
3.	a	b	c	d	e	13.	a	b	c	d	e	23.	a	b	c	d	e	33.	a b c d e
4.	a	b	c	d	e	14.	a	b	c	d	e	24.	a	b	c	d	e	34.	a b c d e
5.	a	b	c	d	e	15.	a	b	c	d	e	25.	a	b	c	d	e	35.	a b c d e
6.	a	b	c	d	e	16.	a	b	c	d	e	26.	a	b	c	d	e	36.	a b c d e
7.	a	b	c	d	e	17.	a	b	c	d	e	27.	a	b	c	d	e	37.	a b c d e
8.	a	b	c	d	e	18.	a	b	c	d	e	28.	a	b	c	d	e	38.	a b c d e
9.	a	b	c	d	e	19.	a	b	c	d	e	29.	a	b	c	d	e	39.	a b c d e
10.	a	b	c	d	e	20.	a	b	c	d	e	30.	a	b	c	d	e	40.	a b c d e

III. DECLARATION

As part of the requirements for achieving **Board Certification in School Crisis Response (CSCR)**, it is necessary that all applicants sign the following statement:

I hereby certify that all information provided in this application packet is accurate and complete. Furthermore, I certify that I personally completed the enclosed examination for **Board Certification in School Crisis Response (CSCR)** and that I received no direct assistance from others. I understand that this Certification aims to identify individuals with extensive knowledge, experience and education related to school crisis response.

I agree to abide by the Academy's Code of Ethical & Professional Standards and agree to hold harmless The American Academy of Experts in Traumatic Stress, Inc. its officers, consultants and employees for any misrepresentation of my credentials and for any malpractice on my part either willful or through negligent conduct, recklessness, and gross misconduct and for all claims, loss, damage, judgment or expense. I understand that The American Academy of Experts in Traumatic Stress does not practice medicine or psychology or provide direct or indirect patient/client care. Furthermore, I understand that **Board Certification in School Crisis Response (CSCR)** does not attest to my ability to treat survivors of traumatic events.

_____   _____
Signature   Date

PLEASE SELECT THE BEST CHOICE FOR THE FOLLOWING QUESTIONS AND MARK YOUR ANSWER ON THE PRECEDING PAGE.

1. According to *A Practical Guide for Crisis Response in Our Schools*, who typically has relationships with many students, can aid in identifying those individuals who are in need of intervention and can coordinate support groups?

   a) Guidance counselor

   b) Social Worker

   c) Teacher

   d) School psychologist

   e) b and d

2. When determining the appropriateness of assembling the school Crisis Response Team, administrators should consider which of the following?

   a) the severity of the event

   b) the number of individuals affected by the event

   c) the reactions of staff members

   d) a and b

   e) all of the above

3. If suicidal thinking is reported by a student, as part of the assessment for suicidal intent, which of the following is (are) most important to evaluate regarding a suicide plan?

   a) the method or means that one would use to commit suicide

   b) the availability or access that one has to a weapon or other method

   c) the lethality or likelihood of success given a chosen suicidal method

   d) the intent or how probable the individual is to follow through on the act

   e) all of the above

4. Which of the following is true concerning *Acute Traumatic Stress Management* (ATSM)?

   a) It is a goal-directed process delivered within the framework of a facilitative or helping attitudinal climate.

   b) It aims to "jump-start" an individual's coping and problem-solving abilities.

   c) It seeks to stabilize acute symptoms of traumatic stress and stimulate healthy, adaptive functioning.

   d) It may increase the likelihood of an individual pursuing mental health intervention, if need be, in the future.

   e) all of the above

5. When initially contacting parents of a child fatally injured in a motor vehicle accident, which of the following should be ascertained?

   a) the events surrounding the child's death

   b) whether funeral arrangements have been made

   c) how much information the parents want disclosed to the school community

   d) a and c

   e) all of the above

6. Which of the following individuals should <u>not</u> be a member of the school Crisis Response Team?

   a) Guidance counselor

   b) Social worker

   c) Principal

   d) Custodian

   e) all may be members of the team

7. What should initially occur when school personnel attempt to address the needs of a substance abusing student?

   a) referral to the Committee on Special Education (CSE)

   b) diagnostic interview

   c) school expulsion or suspension

   d) all of the above

   e) none of the above

8. If you are the first person to be informed of a significant crisis that will likely impact your school, your <u>first</u> course of action should be

   a) Notify your department chairperson

   b) Call the police or fire department

   c) Investigate whether the allegation is credible

   d) Notify the building principal

   e) Telephone your spouse

9. Once you have identified an individual with whom you will implement ATSM, you should

   a) introduce yourself and state your title and/or position.

   b) introduce yourself by name, but avoid using threatening titles and/or positions.

   c) attempt to move the individual away from the stressor if he is medically cleared.

   d) a and c

   e) b and c

10. Following a school crisis, the decision to establish a memorial should only be made by the principal.

    a) True

    b) False

11. According to the National Institute of Mental Health, what are the three leading causes of death among young people 15 to 24 years of age?

    a) homicide, suicide by hanging and drug overdose

    b) gang-related homicide, drug overdose and accidents

    c) automobile accidents, illness and drug overdose

    d) accidents, homicide and suicide

    e) automobile accidents, illness and gang-related homicide

12. The most important variable(s) to assess for when working with survivors of a motor vehicle accident is (are)

    a) the location of the accident

    b) the seriousness of the individual's physical injuries

    c) history of prior psychopathology or traumatization

    d) academic functioning

    e) b and c

13. Mr. Silva, a popular 6th grade teacher, suffered a fatal heat attack while playing tennis on a Sunday afternoon. Which of the following would be the best course of action for notifying staff members?

    a) a mailbox memorandum

    b) an emergency faculty meeting before school

    c) a P.A. announcement

    d) a school-wide assembly

    e) none of the above

14. Acute Traumatic Stress Management (ATSM) focuses on helping people in the aftermath of a tragedy.

    a) True

    b) False

15. It is not necessary to obtain consent from parents of victims if the information to be shared directly involves the emotional well-being of the student population.

    a) True

    b) False

16. Which of the following are "high risk" indicators for acute traumatic stress reactions and chronic stress disorders?

    a) the severity of the event itself

    b) substance involvement

    c) history of mental illness

    d) b and c

    e) all of the above

17. According to *A Practical Guide for Crisis Response in Our Schools*, although teachers are on the front lines in relating with children, they should never intervene with a student in crisis.

    a) True

    b) False

18. Which intervention strategies are most appropriate when addressing the needs of preschool and elementary age children?

    a) Painting

    b) Journal writing

    c) Relaxation techniques

    d) Support groups

    e) all of the above

19. Which of the following is the earliest reaction typically observed in grieving individuals?

    a) Yearning and Searching

    b) Shock

    c) Insomnia

    d) Disorganization

    e) none of the above

20. Generally, as the severity of a traumatic event increases, so does the level of traumatic stress.

    a) True

    b) False

21. Following a tragic automobile accident that took the lives of two high school seniors, the principal provided snacks (i.e., juice and cookies) for groups of students who entered the library to talk. Providing such "goodies" is generally not appropriate and may only serve to reinforce the students' avoidance of classes.

    a) True

    b) False

22. Which has the potential to complicate the bereavement process when an individual believes that he or she should have died with, or instead of, the person who died?

    a) denial

    b) survivor guilt

    c) secondary loss

    d) disorganization

    e) rationalization

23. Following the violent suicide of a 14 year-old boy, the building principal refused to fly the school flag at half-mast or have a tree planted memorializing the young adolescent. He was concerned that such action would glorify the boy's death. The principal's decision is

    a) appropriate

    b) questionable and he should consult with the boy's parents

    c) based upon his own beliefs and he should be more careful not to project these beliefs onto others

    d) b and c

    e) none of the above

24. Factors that affect the grieving process and the acceptance of a loss with preschool and elementary aged children include

    a) history of prior losses

    b) family and social support

    c) the manner in which significant others react to the child

    d) a and c

    e) all of the above

25. Dr. Sefrick, principal of Cedar Hollow Elementary School has achieved Board Certification in School Crisis Response. In a letter to parents following a school crisis, Dr. Sefrick signed his name and then placed the letters, "C.S.C.R. " after his Ed.D. degree. Furthermore, he had the designation, *Board Certified in School Crisis Response*, printed under his title as principal of the school. This action is inappropriate and he should not use the Academy's credential this way.

    a) True

    b) False

26. During which phase of the grieving process do people typically begin to register the reality of a loss and possibly become preoccupied with the lost individual?

    a) Numbing

    b) Disorganization

    c) Reorganization

    d) Bargaining

    e) Yearning & Searching

27. Consider the following statement:

"Many adolescents maintain distorted cognitions regarding their own mortality; that is, they believe that something tragic will never happen to them and that 'good things happen to good people and bad things happen to bad people.' A crisis situation involving death challenges the thoughts that individuals have often developed by this age."

a) This statement is accurate and important to understand

b) This state is partially accurate

c) This statement is inaccurate and jumps to a faulty and dangerous conclusion

d) none of the above

28. Most states have legislation that requires school personnel to report any suspicion of the various forms of child abuse to a child protection agency.

a) True

b) False

29. According to the authors of this publication, students should learn various "red flags" or warning signs regarding violent behavior and they should be informed as to how they can seek assistance within the school if they have concerns over a peer who may become violent.

a) True

b) False

30. Currently, there is no federal law or policy that mandates sex education in the schools.

a) True

b) False

31. Research suggests that traumatic events during childhood:

a) tend to inoculate a child from developing later psychopathology

b) are not correlated with the development of later psychopathology

c) increase the risk for later psychopathology

d) a and b

e) none of the above

32. Which of the following should be avoided by divorcing parents in order to minimize the amount of stress that a young child encounters?

a) forcing the child to take sides in the divorce

b) contact with school staff

c) hostile conversations about the divorce with the child present

d) a and c

e) none of the above

33. According to federal statistics, motor vehicle accidents are the leading cause of death for 15 to 20 year-old individuals.

   a) True

   b) False

34. The most commonly used illicit substance is

   a) Oxycontin

   b) MDMA or "Ecstasy"

   c) Heroin

   d) Marijuana

   e) Crack

35. Andrew was asked by his English teacher to write an essay about an "Aversive Experience." The composition was suggestive of depression and Andrew made references to "not being around anymore." Andrew's teacher referred him to the school psychologist. Which of the following would be advisable for the school psychologist to do?

   a) Ask Andrew if he has been having difficulty sleeping

   b) Assess whether Andrew has a history of alcohol or drug use

   c) Ask Andrew if he has ever tried to harm himself

   d) a and b

   e) all of the above

36. Violent behavior is often the result of numerous contributing factors including faulty learning, poor coping skills, anger, hostility, desire or attempts to control others, peer pressure, exposure to abuse or neglect at home, and psychopathology including depression and impulse control difficulties.

   a) True

   b) False

37. When should a school Crisis Response Team call upon "outside professionals" to intervene?

   a) In the aftermath of a suicide

   b) In the aftermath of an automobile accident

   c) In the aftermath of a gang fight in the cafeteria

   d) When the event overwhelms the Crisis Response Team's ability to respond effectively

   e) all of the above

38. *A Practical Guide for Crisis Response in Our Schools* was written primarily for school administrators and members of school Crisis Response Teams.

    a) True

    b) False

39. Domestic violence includes which of the following?

    a) physical abuse

    b) sexual abuse

    c) psychological abuse

    d) abuse to property and pets

    e) all of the above

40. Which of the following is/are true in the event of a school-based crisis?

    a) The principal should initially meet with the assistant principal and/or the school psychologist in order to determine the appropriateness of assembling the school's Crisis Response Team.

    b) The Crisis Response Team should be immediately brought together in order to prevent a waste of valuable time.

    c) The principal should notify district administration after learning of a school related crisis

    d) a and c

    e) none of the above

About The American Academy of Experts in Traumatic Stress

The American Academy of Experts in Traumatic Stress is a multidisciplinary network of professionals who are committed to the advancement of intervention for survivors of trauma. Our international membership includes individuals from over 200 professions in the health-related fields, emergency services, criminal justice, forensics, law, business and education. The Academy is presently represented by professionals in every state of the United States and over 45 foreign countries.

Society is becoming increasingly aware of the emotional, cognitive and behavioral experience of individuals facing a serious illness or who are exposed to other significant traumatic events. The Academy recognized a need to identify expertise among professionals, across disciplines, and to provide standards for those who regularly work with survivors. Our association is now the largest organization of its kind in the world.

The mission of the Academy is to increase awareness of the effects of trauma and, ultimately, to improve the quality of intervention with survivors. It is in this spirit that we offer:

- Membership/Associate Membership in a prestigious professional association,
- Board Certification Programs,
- Diplomate and Fellow Credentials,
- continuing education credits,
- *Trauma Response*® and *Trauma Response® Infosheets*™, the official publications of the Academy,
- listing in *The International Registry of The American Academy of Experts in Traumatic Stress*™,
- an award winning "guest quarters" on the Internet at **www.traumatic-stress.org**, **www.aaets.org**, **www.atsm.org**, and **www.schoolcrisisresponse.com**,
- an Automated Fax Back System (516) 771-8103, and
- a Code of Ethical & Professional Standards.

Membership

Membership with The American Academy of Experts in Traumatic Stress demonstrates a commitment to the field. It is the first step in a sequential process aimed at identifying expertise among professionals across disciplines. There are four levels of membership in the Academy:

- **Member**

  Members must hold a Doctorate in their field of expertise or hold a Masters Degree and have a minimum of three (3) years experience working with survivors of traumatic events. The Executive Officers reserve the right to grant membership to an individual who does not meet the aforementioned criteria, but who has made important contributions to the field or to the Academy.

- **Associate Member**

  This non-doctoral level of membership is reserved for individuals who have at least two (2) years experience working with survivors of traumatic events. Associate Members are afforded all benefits of membership with the exception of qualifying for the Diplomate credential. However, qualified Associate Members may apply for other Academy certifications.

- **Diplomate**

  Members of the Academy may apply for the designation Board Certified Expert in Traumatic Stress—Diplomate, American Academy of Experts in Traumatic Stress.

  To achieve this credential, a comprehensive application and examination, along with supporting documentation, are utilized in concert to validate a member's experience working with survivors of traumatic events, knowledge of the literature and level of education. The Diplomate credential establishes a much needed standard for professionals, across disciplines, who regularly work with survivors of traumatic events. It is the aim of the Academy to have all of our qualified members achieve Diplomate status.

- **Fellow**

  Fellowship is the highest honor the Academy can bestow upon a member. This designation is awarded to Diplomates who have made significant contributions to the field and to the Academy.

Continuing Education Credits

The Academy awards eight (8) continuing education credits to those members who successfully complete the application/examination process leading to Board Certification and the Diplomate Credential. Additionally, six (6) credits are also awarded to those credentialed experts who complete the evaluative process leading to Fellowship with the Academy.

Publications

Trauma Response® and *Trauma Response® Infosheets*™ are the official publications of the Academy. *Trauma Response*® and *Trauma Response® Infosheets*™ offer members, from diverse specialties, the opportunity to have articles peer reviewed and published.

Certification In Acute Traumatic Stress Management (ATSM)

Certification is awarded to emergency responders who successfully complete the Application & Examination for Certification in Acute Traumatic Stress Management™. The examination is based on *Acute Traumatic Stress Management*™ published by the Academy.

Certification Programs in Traumatic Stress Specialties

All qualified Members and Associate Members of the Academy will have the opportunity to pursue the following credentials:

- Board Certification in Forensic Traumatology™
- Board Certification in Emergency Crisis Response™
- Board Certification in Motor Vehicle Trauma™
- Board Certification in Disability Trauma™
- Board Certification in Pain Management™
- Board Certification in Illness Trauma™
- Board Certification in Bereavement Trauma™
- Board Certification in Domestic Violence™
- Board Certification in Sexual Abuse™
- Board Certification in Rape Trauma™
- Board Certification in Stress Management™
- Board Certification in School Crisis Response™

These programs require candidates to demonstrate extensive knowledge, experience and education specific to each certification area.

The International Registry

All members in good standing are listed in *The International Registry of The American Academy of Experts in Traumatic Stress*™, the association's official directory and referral network. Members who have achieved Board Certification are listed as credentialed experts in the field. The registry is available in bound copy and can also be accessed directly through the Academy's award winning "guest quarters" on the Internet at **www.traumatic-stress.org**.

Credentials

The following are examples of the correct use of The American Academy of Experts in Traumatic Stress' credentials:

- A Member may present his/her status as:

  Robert J. Miller, M.D.

  Member, American Academy of Experts in Traumatic Stress

  Listed in The International Registry of The American Academy of Experts in Traumatic Stress

- A Board Certified Expert — Diplomate may use the following credentials:

  Robert J. Miller, M.D., B.C.E.T.S.

  Board Certified Expert in Traumatic Stress

  Diplomate, American Academy of Experts in Traumatic Stress

  Listed in The International Registry of The American Academy of Experts in Traumatic Stress

- A Fellow (who has achieved Board Certification) may use the following credentials:

  Robert J. Miller, M.D., B.C.E.T.S., F.A.A.E.T.S.

  Board Certified Expert in Traumatic Stress

  Fellow, American Academy of Experts in Traumatic Stress

  Listed in The International Registry of The American Academy of Experts in Traumatic Stress

Members, Associate Members, Diplomates and Fellows who have achieved additional certifications with the Academy in a specialty area may identify themselves with the appropriate credential (e.g., Board Certified in Forensic Traumatology, Board Certified in Emergency Crisis Response, etc.). These professionals may additionally use the respective Academy Credentials, after their educational degree (e.g., Ph.D., B.C.F.T.) or other primary certification (e.g., E.M.T., B.C.E.C.R.), denoting their achievement of specific Academy certifications.

Code of Ethical & Professional Standards

As a multidisciplinary group of professionals, the Academy established a Code of Ethical & Professional Standards for practice across disciplines. All members must adhere to the code.

As a member of The American Academy of Experts in Traumatic Stress, I pledge:

- To be committed to the advancement of intervention for survivors of trauma.
- To maintain the highest standards of competence and professional practice in my work with trauma victims.
- To provide only those services for which I am qualified by virtue of my knowledge, experience and education.
- To maintain my knowledge of the research literature directly related to the services I render.
- To respect the rights of individuals to privacy and confidentiality.
- To never misrepresent my credentials, education or membership status.
- To refrain from conduct that would be adverse to the interest and purpose of the Academy.
- To work toward increasing awareness of traumatic stress and improving intervention with survivors.

Excerpts from *Trauma Response®* Profiles

"The American Academy of Experts in Traumatic Stress fosters awareness. As Sir Francis Bacon said, 'Information is Power.' If we are aware that there is a problem, then there will be people motivated to address the problem. The Academy additionally fosters discovery, innovation, creativity and advancement. And I think that an organization like the Academy helps us strive for raising, to some degree shall I say, the level of quality assurance in the field while promoting creativity and innovation—all with the ultimate goal of being able to better serve people in need."

George S. Everly, Jr., Ph.D., B.C.E.T.S., F.A.A.E.T.S.
Founder & Senior Representative to the United Nations for the International Critical Incident Stress Foundation

"Being an eclectic group is a very great strength because it allows for a cross-pollination of strategies that have been effective in different disciplines.... The Academy has brought together the best and the brightest to work on better understanding of what it is that occurs during traumatic stress and how to advance clinical applications."

Francine Shapiro, Ph.D., B.C.E.T.S.
Originator & Developer of EMDR

"The Academy is a good forum for a variety of professionals to show people (i.e., survivors of traumatic events) that they can cope with the worst kind of adversity or trauma and not upset themselves about it. Now, people in the field who have some "know-how" in working with trauma can be located in the Academy's International Registry—I think that is a good idea."

Albert Ellis, Ph.D., B.C.E.T.S., F.A.A.E.T.S.
Founder, Albert Ellis Institute

"The Academy is a place to go to obtain and share information, and network with others in a multidisciplinary fashion. When I look at The Academy's Board of Advisors and membership, the only word that comes to mind is eclectic and this organization has certainly covered all the bases.... Also, Trauma Response® is outstanding and I believe that every one of the Academy's members looks forward to receiving it."

James T. Reese, Ph.D., B.C.E.T.S., F.A.A.E.T.S.
President, James T. Reese & Associates

"The American Academy of Experts in Traumatic Stress serves a unique and vital purpose. We have to take traumatic stress out of the exclusive domain of psychology and psychiatry. We have to do this! Traumatic stress and its aftermath belong to all of us—medical doctors, lawyers, police departments, psychologists, psychiatrists, teachers, insurance companies, legislators, etc. Education is a crucial step and the issues must be addressed in a public forum."

Beverly J. Anderson, Ph.D., B.C.E.T.S.
President, American Academy of Police Psychology

"Providing an umbrella organization that facilitates dialogue is a valuable service. What the physician, the emergency worker and the psychotherapist have in common and how interventions can be coordinated across disciplines is important. Such a dialogue should result in better treatments for survivors and for those who provide such services."

Donald Meichenbaum, Ph.D.
Clinical Psychologist

"The Academy is multidisciplinary and facilitates different professions coming together under one umbrella. I think that's a great virtue. The cross-pollination that comes from that kind of interaction can only begin to generate a deeper understanding of the phenomenon of traumatic stress as it affects victims and survivors of trauma from all kinds of experience. The Academy provides the opportunity to bring together efforts which allow us to define a mission that transcends ourselves. And in that sense, the Academy, with its diverse and international membership, provides a forum for education, training, publication, and consultation. This not only becomes a national priority or national opportunity, it becomes a potentially global priority of internetting experts in traumatic stress. And I can't think of many things more exciting from my perspective than trying to actualize those objectives which are readily achievable given our technological capacities."

John P. Wilson, Ph.D., B.C.E.T.S., F.A.A.E.T.S.
Founding Member and Past President of the International Society for Traumatic Stress Studies

"One of the Academy's major contributions has to do with the fact that this field is so much bigger than any of the individuals in it. To achieve great things, we need to join resources together and have a multidisciplinary approach. Instead of competing, we need to cooperate. Working together, I think we have greater potential to make a larger impact. No one will listen to a small organization with a few members, but when you have a large organization that cuts across the boundaries of many, many professions, then politicians will listen, governments will listen, the citizens will listen, perhaps a serious difference can be made rather than trying to do this all by one's self. I just don't think it's a good idea to work alone in this field—we need to be allied with one another and assist one another in making progress to do something to mitigate the impact of traumatic stress in people's lives."

Jeffrey T. Mitchell, Ph.D.
President, International Critical Incident Stress Foundation

Committed to the Advancement of Intervention for Survivors of Trauma

The American Academy of Experts in Traumatic Stress®
368 Veterans Memorial Hwy., Commack, NY 11725 • Tel. (516) 543-2217 • Fax (516) 543-6977 • Automated Fax Back System (516) 771-8103 • http://www.aaets.org

The American Academy of Experts in Traumatic Stress®

MEMBERSHIP APPLICATION

Last Name   First Name   M.I.   Title (Dr., Mr., Mrs., Ms.)

Street Address   City   State   Zip Code

Home Telephone (non-published)   Office Telephone(s)   Fax Number

E-mail Address   Highest Educational Degree   Years of Experience in Field

The following list reflects the **professions** of the membership of the Academy at the time of printing. Carefully fill in the boxes corresponding to as many as **three** (3) of your **primary** professions.

- acupuncture
- addiction medicine
- addictionology
- aerospace psychology
- applied psychology
- anesthesiology
- aviation medicine
- bariatric medicine
- behavioral medicine
- bereavement counseling
- biofeedback
- biomedical engineering
- cardiac rehabilitation
- cardiology
- cardiovascular surgery
- career couns./develop.
- child abuse management
- child psychology
- child psychiatry
- chiropractic
- Christian counseling
- clergy
- clinical psychology
- clinical social work
- colon & rectal surgery
- community health
- community psychology
- community trauma intervention
- coroner
- corrections officer
- counseling
- counseling psychology
- court interpreter
- criminal justice
- crisis intervention
- critical incident debrief.
- critical care
- cross cultural psychiatry
- dentistry
- disability evaluation

- disability management
- disability medicine
- disaster relief
- disaster response
- diving medicine
- divorce mediation
- economist
- education
- EMDR
- emergency med. services
- emergency medicine
- emergency psychiatry
- emergency services
- employee assistance
- endocrinology
- family medicine
- female psychology
- fire service
- flight nursing
- flight surgery
- forensic dentistry
- forensic medicine
- forensic odontology
- forensic pathology
- forensic psychiatry
- forensic psychology
- forensic science
- forensic traumatology
- gastroenterology
- general medicine
- geriatric medicine
- gerontology
- geropsychology
- gynecology
- hand surgery
- health education
- health law & policy
- health psychology
- holistic healing
- holistic medicine

- homeopathic med.
- hostage negotiation
- human factors engineering
- hypnosis
- injury prevention
- insurance medicine
- integrative medicine
- intensive care med.
- internal medicine
- journalism
- law
- legal medicine
- liability management
- marriage & family ther.
- massage therapy
- media psychology
- mediation
- medical oncology
- medical psychology
- medical psychother.
- medical writer
- motor vehicle trauma
- military chaplaincy
- military medicine
- military psychology
- mind-body integration
- mind-body medicine
- mind-body therapy
- ministry
- muscle therapy
- music therapy
- natural disaster trauma
- NLP
- neonatology
- nephrology
- neurobehavioral toxicology
- neurologic surgery
- neurological rehab.
- neurology
- neuropsychology

- neurosurgery
- nuclear medicine
- nursing
- nursing administration
- nursing education
- nutrition
- obstetrics
- occupational medicine
- ophthalmology
- oral & maxillo-facial surg.
- orthopedic surgery
- osteopathic & holistic med.
- pain management
- pain medicine
- parapsychology
- pastoral counseling
- pathology
- peace psychology
- pediatrics
- penologic medicine
- pharmacology
- pharmacy
- physiatry
- physical medicine
- physical therapy
- physical trainer
- physician assistant
- plastic & recon. surgery
- podiatric medicine
- police officer
- police psychology
- preventative medicine
- professor
- psychiatric nursing
- psychiatry
- psychoanalysis
- psychobiology
- psychodramatist
- psychohistory
- psycho-oncology

- psychopharmacology
- psychotherapy
- public health administra.
- pulmonary medicine
- pulmonary rehabilitation
- rehabilitation
- rehabilitation medicine
- rehabilitation psychology
- respiratory therapy
- school counseling
- school psychology
- sex therapy
- social work
- spiritual psychotherapy
- speech-language pathol.
- sports medicine
- sports psychology
- substance abuse testing
- suicideology
- surgery
- surgical critical care
- surgical pathology
- thoracic surgery
- toxicology
- transpersonal hypnotherapy
- transpersonal psychology
- trauma surgery
- trauma therapy
- traumatology
- trial advocacy
- trial attorney
- trigger point myotherapy
- veterinary medicine
- vocational counseling
- war surgery
- other: _____

All members will have the opportunity to provide additional information (e.g., areas of specialization) for *The International Registry*, the Academy's official membership directory and referral network. I wish to apply for:

☐ **Membership**
Membership with The American Academy of Experts in Traumatic Stress demonstrates a commitment to the advancement of intervention for survivors of trauma. Members must hold a Doctorate in their field of expertise or hold a Masters Degree and have a minimum of three (3) years experience working with survivors of traumatic events. All members of the Academy will receive a copy of the Academy's *Application & Examination for Board Certification and the Diplomate Credential.* Qualified Members may additionally apply for other Academy certifications. Annual dues payment for membership is **$ 125.**

☐ **Associate Membership**
Associate Membership with The American Academy of Experts in Traumatic Stress demonstrates a commitment to the advancement of intervention for survivors of trauma. This non-doctoral level of membership is reserved for individuals who have at least two (2) years experience working with survivors of traumatic events. Associate Members are afforded all benefits of membership with the exception of qualifying for the Diplomate Credential. However, qualified Associate Members may apply for other Academy certifications. Annual dues payment for associate membership is **$ 80.**

Please send me information about the Academy's other certification programs:

☐ BOARD CERTIFICATION IN FORENSIC TRAUMATOLOGY™
☐ BOARD CERTIFICATION IN EMERGENCY CRISIS RESPONSE™
☐ BOARD CERTIFICATION IN MOTOR VEHICLE TRAUMA™
☐ BOARD CERTIFICATION IN DISABILITY TRAUMA™

☐ BOARD CERTIFICATION IN PAIN MANAGEMENT™
☐ BOARD CERTIFICATION IN ILLNESS TRAUMA™
☐ BOARD CERTIFICATION IN BEREAVEMENT TRAUMA™
☐ BOARD CERTIFICATION IN DOMESTIC VIOLENCE™

☐ BOARD CERTIFICATION IN SEXUAL ABUSE™
☐ BOARD CERTIFICATION IN RAPE TRAUMA™
☐ BOARD CERTIFICATION IN STRESS MANAGEMENT™
☐ BOARD CERTIFICATION IN SCHOOL CRISIS RESPONSE™

Membership dues payment **must** accompany this application. Please make personal/company check (from an American Bank only) payable to **The American Academy of Experts in Traumatic Stress, Inc.** Upon approval of the Executive Officers, an elegant membership/associate membership certificate, suitable for framing, will be forwarded to you and you will begin receiving *Trauma Response*® and *The Academy Update*™, the Academy's official publications.

I certify that the information provided on this application is accurate and complete:

Signature   Date

Enclosed is my check for $_____ or please charge $_____ to my ☐ VISA   ☐ American Express   ☐ MasterCard   ☐ Discover Card

Account No.   Expiration Date   Signature   Date

The American Academy of Experts in Traumatic Stress®

Administrative Offices, 368 Veterans Memorial Highway, Commack, New York 11725
Tel. (631) 543-2217 • Fax (631) 543-6977 • Automated Fax Back System (516) 771-8103
www.schoolcrisisresponse.com • www.traumatic-stress.org. • www.atsm.org
FEDERAL IDENTIFICATION NO. 11-3285203

ORDER FORM

A PRACTICAL GUIDE FOR CRISIS RESPONSE IN OUR SCHOOLS
———— Fifth Edition ————

Name (Including Title): _____

Position: _____

School District: _____

Street Address: _____

City: _____

State & Zip Code: _____

Tel. No.: _____

Fax. No.: _____

PLEASE ASSIST THE ACADEMY IN KNOWING OTHER EDUCATORS
WHO MAY BE INTERESTED IN PURCHASING THIS PUBLICATION.

Name (Including Title): _____

Position: _____

School District: _____

Street Address: _____

City: _____

State & Zip Code: _____

Paperback 8 ½ x 11, 140 pages
ISBN 0-9674762-3-2
$24.95 US + S&H

Shipping & Handling
All orders are processed and shipped within 24 hours.
<u>United States</u>
Priority Mail: $5.00 first book, $1.00 for each additional book
For orders over 25, call the Academy at (631) 543-2217.
<u>Canada & Foreign</u>
Air Mail: $6.00 first book, $1.50 for each additional book

Purchase Orders
Purchase orders are accepted from organizations and
governmental agencies. The Academy's Fed. I.D. No. is 11-3285203.

Credit Card Orders
American Express, VISA, MasterCard or Discover Card are accepted.
Please telephone the Academy at (631) 543-2217.

Checks
Please make checks payable to:
The American Academy of Experts in Traumatic Stress.

Orders from Libraries & the Book Trade
Libraries, bookstores and other resellers, please contact the Academy at
(631) 543-2217 for pricing and discount information.

	Quantity	Price
$24.95 U.S. Funds	_____	_____
For orders over 25, deduct 20%	_____	_____
Shipping & Handling		_____
TOTAL AMOUNT		_____

For Credit Card Orders:

Please charge $_____ to my ☐ VISA ☐ American Express ☐ MasterCard ☐ Discover Card

Account No. _____   Expiration Date _____   Signature _____   Date _____

Please send this order form and your check or money order (i.e., Payable in U.S. Funds) to:
The American Academy of Experts in Traumatic Stress
Administrative Offices
368 Veterans Memorial Highway
Commack, New York 11725

THIS FORM MAY BE FAXED DIRECTLY TO THE ACADEMY'S ADMINISTRATIVE OFFICES FOR IMMEDIATE PROCESSING.
FAX: (631) 543-6977